# HOBBES'S *LEVIATHAN*

**Continuum Reader's Guides**

*Aristotle's* Nicomachean Ethics – Christopher Warne

*Heidegger's* Being and Time – William Blattner

*Hume's* Enquiry Concerning Human Understanding – Alan Bailey and Dan O'Brien

*Hume's* Dialogues Concerning Natural Religion – Andrew Pyle

*Nietzsche's* Genealogy of Morals – Daniel Conway

*Plato's* Republic – Luke Purshouse

*Wittgenstein's* Tractatus Logico Philosophicus – Roger M.White

# HOBBES'S *LEVIATHAN*
## *Reader's Guide*

### LAURIE M. JOHNSON BAGBY

continuum

To my husband Tim Bagby

Continuum International Publishing Group
The Tower Building                      80 Maiden Lane
11 York Road                            Suite 704
London SE1 7NX                          New York, NY 10038

© Laurie M. Johnson Bagby 2007

First published 2007

Laurie M. Johnson Bagby has asserted her right under the Copyright,
Designs and Patents Act, 1988, to be identified as Author of this work

**British Library Cataloguing-in-Publication Data**
A catalogue record for this book is available from the British Library.

ISBN – 10: 0 8264 8619 3 (hardback) 0 8264 8620 7 (paperback)
ISBN – 13: 978 0 8264 8619 6 (hardback) 978 0 8264 8620 2 (paperback)

**Library of Congress Cataloguing-in-Publication Data**
A catalog record for this book is available from the Library of Congress.

Typeset by Servis Filmsetting Ltd, Manchester
Printed and bound in Great Britain by Cromwell Press Ltd,
Trowbridge, Wiltshire

# CONTENTS

# ACKNOWLEDGEMENTS

I would like to thank Ms Kathy MacKenzie, my graduate research assistant, for all her help looking up books and articles and helping with the bibliography and other editorial work. Her work has been exceptional and her help has been invaluable. Also, I would like to thank Professor Marsha Frey, a historian at Kansas State University, for reading the text and providing useful critiques and suggestions on the history content in this book. Thanks to my husband Tim and my son Hunter, and to my parents Ken and Nina Johnson for their patience, understanding and support.

All quotations for Hobbes's *Leviathan* are taken from Michael Oakeshott's edition (see Guide to Further Reading for more information on this edition).

# CHAPTER 1

# CONTEXT AND INTRODUCTION

From a certain perspective, Thomas Hobbes did not get a very good start in life. But from another angle, his misfortune as a boy contributed to his future success. Emphasizing the importance of fear in his political theory, Hobbes wrote in his autobiography that on 5 April 1588, he and fear were born twins. This was because his mother, knowing the Spanish Armada was sailing up the English Channel, gave premature birth to him. But the real source of his misfortune was not the Spanish Armada (which was defeated) or his mother, but his father.

Hobbes's father, who was also named Thomas, was an Anglican minister from Malmesbury (Westport). He was poor, uneducated, probably an alcoholic, and he had a reputation for being irresponsible. Once, he was brought before a church court 'for want of quarter sermons and for not catechisinge the younge'.[1] The following year, he was accused of slandering a neighbouring vicar, Richard Jeane, and was required to make an act of penitence in Jeane's church. When he did not do this and also did not pay the associated fine, he was excommunicated. Finally, Hobbes's father abandoned his family when Hobbes was 16, after a fight with Jeane in front of his own church.[2] He physically assaulted Jeane, and 'was forcd to fly for it', and died 'in obscurity beyound London' to avoid the police (Aubrey 1950: 148). After he fled to London, nothing further was heard from him.

Hobbes's mother, left on her own to care for him and his younger sister and older brother, turned for aid to Francis Hobbes, a wealthy uncle. Francis was also of Malmesbury, and had no children of his own. He was a glover by trade, wealthy, and a 'burgess and an alderman (the chief magistrate of the town)' (Martinich 1999: 5). He paid the family's expenses and sent Hobbes to primary school. After attending another school in Malmesbury, Hobbes then graduated to a school in Westport. There he learned from a favourite teacher, Robert Latimer, how to read and translate ancient Greek and Latin. Although Hobbes moved away from these humanistic studies in his mature work, the influence of his school days with Latimer remained with him (Martinich 1999: 7).

With the financial help of his uncle, Hobbes was able to attend college at Magdalen Hall, Oxford. He graduated in 1608, his future reasonably secure. Perhaps Hobbes's uncle would have provided such an education for Thomas even if his father had not abandoned the family. However, at the very least, we can say that Hobbes no doubt personally benefited by the substitution of his father's influence and example for those of his uncle Francis, despite the pain that his father's actions no doubt caused him, his siblings, and his mother.

While at Oxford, Hobbes studied subjects such as grammar, rhetoric, logic, and physics (Martinich 1999: 8–18). He was also employed by the family of young William Cavendish (the future Earl of Devonshire). He would be William's tutor and tour guide on European excursions. Even after William died in 1629, Hobbes continued to serve the Cavendish family, its relatives and friends, throughout his life. They in turn acted as his sponsors and allowed him plenty of scope for contemplation and writing. He worked not only as tutor to William and other young men but also as a secretary and financial advisor to the family. This type of employment was not uncommon for intellectuals like Hobbes who wished to live as scholars instead of following the typical path of career and family. Indeed, Hobbes did not marry and, so far as we know, had no children.

Hobbes never discontinued his education. Actually, as is often the case, his most meaningful education occurred after he left college. He served as a guide, travelling throughout Europe with William and other young men in his charge. He travelled between 1610 and 1615 to Venice, Paris, and other great cities, where he was able to meet and converse with the likes of Galileo, Bacon, Gassendi, and Descartes. To a certain extent, Hobbes was still interested in the ideas and priorities of humanism, the prevailing school of thought. Hobbes was attracted to its growing scepticism about the efficacy of moral values and the prevalence of self-interest in human nature. He pleased his fellow intellectuals with his first published work, a translation of Thucydides' *History of the Peloponnesian War*. From Thucydides he drew the conclusion that moral values without the backing of force are of no consequence. But he also drew from it and from his life experience the idea that democracy was not a viable option. His conclusion in favour of absolutism separated his ideas from those of his fellow intellectuals who preferred republican government.

Influenced especially by the example of Galileo, whom he met in 1636, Hobbes was more impressed by natural science and Euclidean geometry than he was by moral theory and metaphysics. Because of their promise of certainty, he turned to these fields for models about how to think about the social world. Regarding his deep respect for geometry, the biographer Aubrey wrote:

> He was 40 yeares old before he looked on Geometry; which happened accidentally. Being in a Gentleman's Library, Euclid's Elements lay open, and 'twas the 47 *El. Libri* I. He read the Proposition. *By* G----, sayd he (he would now and then sweare an emphaticall Oath by way of emphasis) *this is impossible!* So he reads the Demonstration of it, which referred him back to such a Proposition; which proposition he read. That referred him back to another, which he also read. *Et sic deincepts* [and so on] that at last he was demonstratively convinced of that trueth. This made him in love with Geometry. (Aubrey: 150)

According to some, Hobbes did not become the master of geometry, but he nevertheless remained impressed and used its model of reasoning well (Grant 1990). He was also influenced by the emerging theory that what people know about their world is filtered through the untrustworthy experience of their senses. In his view, this unfortunate fact kept human discourse in the realm of competing opinions instead of knowledge. There was a way out of the morass of competing perceptions and opinions, however. Hobbes would employ the methods of science and mathematics to arrive at basic definitions of politically relevant ideas, which could then be the basis for agreement on social and political matters (Grant 1990). This became his life project – to make the treatment of political problems more like a science, and to erect upon a solid scientific foundation an effective and lasting political order which produced peace.

Hobbes's project became even more crucial to him because of certain events during his lifetime, events which in his view were ruinous to England, which led to the execution of a king (Charles I), and the temporary demise of the English monarchy. By 1640 the power of the English parliament had grown to the point where it could challenge the king's authority. A new set of interests had emerged within parliament. There were now many members who dissented from the established Church of England. They wanted to eliminate the authority of the bishops who buttressed the king's power, and thus take more power for themselves. On the other hand, royalists generally favoured the traditional idea of divine right (the idea that God gives the king his right to rule) and supported the Church of England and the king.

Religious controversy had been brewing in England long before Hobbes was born. King Henry VIII established the Church of England in 1533, separating his kingdom from the authority of the Catholic church. The church had stood in the way of his divorce from Catherine of Aragon and his political ambitions, and so in his view it was the church that provoked his extraordinary reaction. Previously, Henry had expressed his absolute loyalty to the pope and church and his loathing for Protestant ideas. But when Henry created the Church of England for his own selfish reasons, the Protestants were consequently strengthened. And it is understandable that they soon turned to questioning the government's right to impose the Church of England on them, just as they had questioned the primacy of the Catholic church. At the same time, and just as naturally, they disputed the king's authority over their political and economic affairs.

James I, who ruled in Hobbes's young adulthood (1603–1625), supported the Church of England, and he too claimed a 'divine right' to rule. However, the Protestants in the House of Commons questioned the validity of this 'divine right' as well as the spiritual authority of the official church. They also began to complain about important issues such as arbitrary taxation, claiming that the monarch should have no power to tax citizens without the approval of parliament. James's son, Charles I (1625–1649), inherited an increasingly uncooperative parliament, and so he simply decided to disband it. He did not allow parliament to meet at all between 1629 and 1640. Unfortunately for his future, Charles decided to try to impose upon the Presbyterian Scots the English Book of Common Prayer. The Scots took up arms against England, making their point that they would not accept such an imposition. With the Scots in revolt, Charles found it necessary to call for parliament's assistance to raise taxes for the war. The result was a disaster for his reign.

Presbyterians had become prominent in the English parliament, and many sided with the Scots' cause instead of supporting the king. They wanted to limit the power of the king, especially to stop him from granting toleration to Catholics, and they wanted to expand their own power. As soon as parliament met in 1640, its first order of business was to make demands designed to weaken the king's authority. In his commentary on these times, *Behemoth*, Hobbes put it this way:

> And therefore the King found not the more, but the less help from this parliament: and most of the members thereof, in their ordinary discourses, seemed to wonder why the King should make a war upon Scotland; and in that parliament sometimes called them their brethren the Scots. But instead of taking the King's business, which was the raising of money, into their consideration, they fell upon the redressing of grievances, and especially such ways of levying money as in the late intermission of parliaments the King had been forced to use . . .
> (Hobbes 1990: 32)

The parliament raised an army of the loyal nobility and gentry to fight the Scots, but this step fed the mistrust and hostility between king and parliament. When the king did not heed the demands of the dissenters, parliament imprisoned some of the king's ministers, and forced others to flee. Also, dissenters raised suspicions that the queen, who was a Catholic, was trying to bring her religion back to favour. The country descended towards civil war.

The struggle between the king and parliament was protracted, and began with legal arguments, petitions, and declarations asserting the independence and supremacy of parliament over the king. But Charles refused time and again to grant these petitions, responding with legal arguments of his own. Hobbes says of this time, 'Hitherto, though it were a war before, yet there was no blood shed; they shot at one another nothing but paper' (Hobbes 1990: 109). But, like the king, the leaders of parliament began to raise their own army, first led by the Earl of Essex, then by Sir Thomas Fairfax.

The civil war began in earnest in 1642, and eventually the dissenters got the upper hand. Hobbes was horrified when he learned in France (where he had fled from the strife) that the opposition forces had captured Charles in 1648 and executed him in 1649. While in Paris, Hobbes had the privilege of tutoring the king's son, young Charles II, in mathematics; the boy too was in exile, having escaped the violence that killed his father.[3] After the king's capture, Oliver Cromwell (previously Fairfax's lieutenant-general and already something of a war hero) came to the fore as a political leader, appealing in particular to the more radical Protestant sects that were well represented in the army but only somewhat in parliament. Hobbes lists these religious elements as 'Brownists, Anabaptists, Independents, Fifth-monarchy-men, Quakers, and divers others, all commonly called by the name of fanatics: insomuch as there was no so dangerous an enemy to the Presbyterians, as this brood of their own hatching' (Hobbes 1990: 136).

From 1649 to 1653 England was a Commonwealth, and then from 1653 to 1660, the government became a 'Protectorate' under Cromwell's direct rule. After Cromwell's death, it was briefly in the hands of his son Richard, who was much less competent and who abdicated his leadership in 1659. Hobbes's interpretation of the time of the Commonwealth and Protectorate was that pride and 'vainglory' drove the men in parliament and later Cromwell and his followers to try to assert their supremacy over the crown and the people.[4] He especially targeted firebrand Presbyterian and other dissenting ministers, and the educated gentlemen who supported them, for abandoning their duty to teach the people order and obedience:

> And as these [ministers] did in the pulpit draw the people to their opinions, and to a dislike of the Church-government, Canons, and Common-prayer book, so did the other [gentlemen] make them in love with democracy by their harangues in the parliament, and by their discourses and communication with people in the country, continually extolling liberty and inveighing against tyranny, leaving the people to collect of themselves that this tyranny was the present government of the state. (Hobbes 1990: 23)

Hobbes did not believe in the ideals of these rebels, and he did not think *they* truly believed their ideals either. Instead, he wrote that they were driven by their own vanity and desire for power (what Hobbes so often called 'vainglory'). They preached a Christian duty to disobey the king's commands on how to worship. Of this development, Hobbes wrote wryly, 'men do, for the most part, rather draw the Scripture to their own sense, than follow the true sense of the Scripture. . .' (Hobbes 1990: 51). At the heart of this arrogance, in Hobbes's view, lay the universities, which had become hotbeds of criticism and dissent, inspired by the philosophies and histories of ancient Greece and Rome so prominently taught and held up as the pinnacle of learning. In the universities and in the pulpits of many churches, Hobbes saw arrogant men bent on self-glorification, not principled men willing to risk themselves for the truth (Shulman 1988). The ministers spread the most dangerous doctrine of all to the common people – that scripture, or religious conviction, could justify open rebellion against a lawful monarch – and all for their own empowerment.

The Commonwealth failed (in Hobbes's view) due to the incompetence and the competition of its members, and in its place was erected a bald-faced dictatorship under Cromwell, who tried to impose puritanical religious and moral laws on a weary population. After all this strife, Hobbes said, the English people realized that hereditary monarchy was better than the disasters created by the demand for popular choice. The people elected a largely royalist and Anglican parliament in the wake of their disappointment with Cromwell's rule. This parliament called for the return of Charles II to the throne under certain conditions, including amnesty for all dissenters. But Charles's reign was not friendly to dissenting Protestants, and he was even accused of favouring Catholics and perhaps secretly adhering to the Catholic faith himself.

From the standpoint of someone who desired a more representative system of government, the experiment of the Commonwealth might have seemed like progress, even if it ultimately failed. Charles II had to contend with a stronger and more assertive parliament, even if it was now generally supportive of him. This progress was made much more secure in the Glorious Revolution of 1688, when the power of the monarchy was limited still further by the Bill of Rights, and the Act of Toleration (1689) granted dissenting Protestants freedom of worship. However, at the time when he was developing his arguments for *Leviathan*, Hobbes could have had no idea that the future of England might include a strong parliament without risk of chaos and civil war. Indeed, he died before the events of the Glorious Revolution took place. It was his experience of the English Civil War and his reaction to it that set the stage for the writing of *Leviathan* and its publication in 1651.

Hobbes was convinced that vanity and pride were behind all con-
flicting points of view, especially the religious and political opinions
that caused most of the disorder of his time. Because of his experience, he did not believe that people could be taught to tolerate
different religious perspectives. At the same time, Hobbes did not
think that many of the religious beliefs and practices that people
argued about could be prove true or false or that these arguments
even really mattered.[5] This led him to conclude that the imposition
of a single church and set of religious practices was not only acceptable but desirable for practical, political (and not spiritual) reasons.
He argued that Christians could in good conscience accept any doctrine or worship style imposed upon them by the crown. In fact, he
concluded that the only effective way out of the conflict caused by
pride and various points of view was the absolute imposition of the
will of one sovereign on all subjects and all contentious issues. For
Hobbes, it was clear that even what many would call tyranny was
preferable to the uncertainty and violence of civil war.

# CHAPTER 2

# OVERVIEW OF THEMES

The monster leviathan appears in the Bible's *Book of Job*, where it is depicted as a beast created by God and used by God as proof of his infinite power. It appears in chapter 40 of *Job* when God is answering Job's plea for an explanation for his misfortunes. God first mentions the creature behemoth (the title of another of Hobbes's books, that one being about the English Civil War). He tells Job, 'Behold the behemoth I made with thee', and goes on to describe a huge ox-like beast. He describes the beast as incredibly strong. It is something Job could never control, and which only God can control. Then God says, 'Canst thou draw out the leviathan with a hook? Or canst thou tie his tongue with a cord? Canst thou put a ring in his nose, or bore through his jaw with a buckle?' (Job 40.20–21).[1] God ends his description of leviathan with this pithy statement, meant to drive home to Job His immense power: 'There is no power upon the earth that can be compared with him who was made to fear no one. He beholdeth every high thing. He is king over all the children of pride' (Job 41.24–25).

Whatever the leviathan is (some people imagine it as a huge crocodile), it is extremely powerful, something that God made and only God can control. That is strange, because in Hobbes's masterpiece, the leviathan is not a monster created by God but rather an 'artificial person' created by man in order to serve very human purposes. It is extremely powerful and one of its chief purposes is to be 'king over all the children of pride'. But it is a human creation, certainly not of divine origin. The title page of the first edition of *Leviathan* features a picture of a sovereign – a giant human being with a crown on his head, within whom is depicted myriad smaller humans. The sovereign's 'body' is thus depicted as being made up of countless other human beings.[2]

The famous first edition illustration depicts in a nutshell Hobbes's preferred view of government: it is created by and for human beings, and it is made up of them. But human beings cannot be sovereign over themselves. Instead, they are subordinate to a greater power which must direct them if they are to be successful and happy. Hobbes begins his book with an introduction and immediately claims that man, through his skill or art, can imitate God's nature by making an 'artificial animal'. He goes on to say that the greatest of human art produces the most powerful such animal, the 'artificial man' known as the sovereign, 'that great LEVIATHAN called a COMMONWEALTH, or STATE, in Latin CIVITAS. . .' (19).

Hobbes then compares the various parts of the state to parts of the human body – sovereignty itself is the artificial soul of the state. Magistrates and officers are the joints, reward and punishment the nerves, etc. To make his point clear, at the end of this description, Hobbes makes a comparison between the way human beings make this artificial man and the way that God makes things: 'Lastly, the *pacts* and *covenants*, by which the parts of this body politic were at first made, set together, and united, resemble that *fiat*, or the *let us make man*, pronounced by God at the creation' (19).

Hobbes is commenting on the extraordinary power of *man*, not God. Man's ability to make pacts and covenants is somehow arbitrary in the same way that God's creative acts are arbitrary – that is, these pacts and covenants require no higher explanation or justification. Man's power is or can be absolute on earth. It turns out that, in Hobbes's view, God's power is not as great on earth as it is in heaven, at least for now. Man can and should have godlike power over his situation. In particular, through the creation of a godlike absolute sovereign, mankind can escape from the violence which stops human progress and happiness.

Hobbes recommends that people submit themselves almost completely to the will of a sovereign power, a will which represents thereafter the people's will. Unlike future liberal thinkers who wanted to put a limit on the power of the sovereign and even, as with Locke, wanted to argue that people should be able to dissolve or revolt against a tyrannical government, Hobbes wants people to see the logic of submitting to a sovereign of almost limitless power. He wants them to accept his authority willingly, even if that authority is not always pleasantly applied.

Once having agreed to the social contract, people will have no right to revolt against their government, no right even to complain. The only right which the people will retain is the right to try to protect their own lives if they are threatened with death. In Hobbes's view, no one can take away this right to self-preservation in any case – it represents the survival instinct and it is the whole reason for entering into the social contract in the first place. But the individual right to fight back is not the same as the right to revolution. It simply means that if anyone, including the government, comes to take away your life, you have the right to resist. This is because your chief interest, naturally, is in survival. If you manage to escape, good for you. If you do not escape, the sovereign power can and will capture and kill you – and is perfectly within *its* rights to do so.

Hobbes believed that if people thought they had the right to judge whether or not the government was just, and to reject all or part of it, social and civil chaos would ensue. As we will see, that is why he complained so much about Aristotelian political philosophy, which encouraged the idea that there was such a thing as unjust government. This is also why he did not like the Catholic church, or any religious perspective which sought to judge government and presumed to tell the people whether laws were just or unjust. To assign to individuals the power to make such judgements was to invite conflict with the government or among factions within the state. The worst possible consequence of such presumptuousness, the one to avoid at all costs, was civil war, because such conflict brings the distinct possibility of violent death, which for Hobbes was the worst evil. He would definitely disagree with the Cold War slogan of American patriots 'better dead than red'.

Hobbes outlines his agenda in his introduction. It is 'to describe the nature of this artificial man. . .' the sovereign (19). To this end he constructs his book in four parts: 'First, [to describe] the *matter* thereof, and the *artificer*; both which is *man*.

Secondly, *how*, and by what *covenants* it is made; what are the *rights* and just *power* or *authority* of a *sovereign*; and what it is that *preserveth* and *dissolveth* it.

Thirdly, what is a *Christian commonwealth*.

Lastly, what is the *kingdom of darkness*' (19).

In his introduction, Hobbes only briefly comments on his first argument. In one very memorable sentence, he argues that in order to understand man (human nature), all we have to do is honestly examine ourselves. When we examine ourselves without blinking, what we see will not be pleasant, but it will be true. We will find the same passions in ourselves as all other people experience, although each individual's passions are directed at objects he or she personally values – there is no collective definition of the good which can sway us from our selfish preferences.

The latter observation is very important for understanding why Hobbes thinks we need an absolute sovereign instead of some kind of democratic system. We are all passionate creatures, but we are all passionate about different things. We, as individuals, have peculiar aims and desires; all of our feelings refer back to our own individual perspectives driven by those desires. If it is true that human beings are naturally rather individualistic, then we could never agree on something as important as what constitutes justice unless someone forced us to agree. This is precisely what Hobbes thinks is the role of a proper government – to force outward agreement and conformity so that the peace is kept.

The first part of *Leviathan*, 'Of Man', is about human nature. Hobbes will draw upon not only common-sense experience, but also on what he considers to be scientific explanations about our physical bodies and our physical peculiarities which set us apart from one another. Here Hobbes will try to prove that it is impossible for two people to agree fully with one another, let alone for a whole commonwealth to agree, hence in his view the obvious need for an absolute sovereign. Here he will also introduce us to the state of nature, in which human nature unchecked provokes chaos and radical insecurity. Finally, Hobbes tries to show how passions and superstition block people's ability to see where their true interests lie: in submission and peace.

*Leviathan*'s second part, 'Of Commonwealth', explains Hobbes's ideas on the rights of nature and laws of nature, and their relationship to civil society. Hobbes develops his famous social contract, in which each individual agrees to give up his or her right to self-preservation in nature and hand over all authority to a sovereign power, where it becomes irrevocable. This second part would not make sense unless the reader accepts Hobbes's view of human nature developed in Part I. If humans can be guided by more rational agreement, and we can generally assume goodwill, then it is possible to contemplate a stable democracy or mixed form of government. But Hobbes calls such democratic ideas 'absurd', and spends quite a bit of time in this section making the case that only absolute monarchy makes sense, if what we want is peace. In Hobbes's view, peace is the paramount good from which all other goods flow.

The third part of *Leviathan*, 'Of a Christian Commonwealth', deals with how Christianity can be made compatible with absolute monarchy. In order to answer this question fully, Hobbes constructs his own Christian theology, his own reading of the Bible, and his own interpretation of the proper relationship between church and state. His aim is to make it clear that Christianity does not necessitate judgement or criticism of the state, no matter what the state does or orders its citizens to do. In other words, Hobbes tries to prove that one can be a good Christian and not object to the laws and orders of government, even if those laws and orders seem to defy Christian beliefs and morality. Instead, Hobbes argues that Christians' only duty relative to the state is obedience. If the state sins, it is the responsibility of the sovereign, not the citizens. Hobbes also wants to make it clear that the church itself must be subordinate to the sovereign for the same reason – power and authority cannot be divided or there will be civil breakdown leading to the violence Hobbes so wants to avoid. Hobbes tries to show that the Bible supports the subordination of church to state.

In the final part of *Leviathan*, 'Of the Kingdom of Darkness', Hobbes tackles ideas that get in the way of his political agenda, especially Catholic ideas that place church above state and promote belief in otherworldly things. Hobbes particularly dislikes beliefs in things that are not physical and cannot be proven, and the more mysterious they are the more he dislikes them. What Hobbes would call superstitions entice a person's attention away from this-worldly concerns and makes him value transcendent things more than those things he can control. Superstitious beliefs encourage disobedience to earthly powers. Catholic beliefs particularly encourage disobedience because of the earthly arrangement of the Catholic church, with its pope and its government-like structure, as well as its overt claim at that time to earthly authority over monarchs. Although he does challenge these beliefs quite strongly in other parts of his book, Hobbes develops that challenge more completely here. His sarcastic side is never stronger than it is in this part of *Leviathan*, and so this part gives a special insight into the way Hobbes thought. Finally, he gives us a very useful 'Review, and Conclusion', in which he attempts to summarize, supplement, and defend his most important points.

# CHAPTER 3

# READING THE TEXT

The first part of Hobbes's *Leviathan* is 'Of Man', and within that first part there are sixteen chapters. Some would say it is the second most important part of the book (with Part II, 'Of Commonwealth', being the most important). But in some ways, it is the most important because it supplies Hobbes's assumptions. Since Hobbes is making the utmost effort to be scientific in his approach to what many consider to be a subject intractable to science, we should look very carefully at his assumptions and the definitions he builds on in this chapter. 'Of Man' is all about human nature, especially about how human beings perceive, think, and react. Hobbes begins with a discussion of the human senses. Sense is of course a physical thing, and sense is in Hobbes's view the origin of all our perceptions and thoughts. In this first chapter, Hobbes argues that our perceptions and thoughts are simply by-products of the physical processes of sensation (in Peters 1967: Ch. 6):

> The cause of sense, is the external body, or object, which presseth the organ proper to each sense, either immediately, as in the taste and touch; or mediately, as in seeing, hearing, and smelling; which pressure, by the mediation of the nerves, and other strings and membranes of the body, continued inwards to the brain and heart, causeth there a resistance, or counter-pressure, or endeavour of the heart to deliver itself, which endeavour, because *outward*, seemeth to be some matter without. . . . Neither in us that are pressed, are they any thing else, but divers motions; for motion produceth nothing but motion. But their appearance to us is fancy, the same waking, that dreaming. And as pressing, rubbing, or

striking the eye, makes us fancy a light; and pressing the ear, produceth a din; so do the bodies also we see, or hear, produce the same by their strong, though unobserved action. For if these colours and sounds were in the bodies, or objects that cause them, they could not be severed from them, as by glasses, and in echoes by reflection, we see they are . . . (21–22)

This way of starting a discussion of human nature may seem esoteric, but actually it is right to the point and very significant. Hobbes is taking issue, as he makes clear in the last paragraph of this first chapter, with the 'universities of Christendom', whose arguments about how we know things, tended to rely heavily on the writings of Aristotle. Hobbes is pointing out the more modern scientific view that what we perceive through our senses is not the same as what causes our sensations. We see a particular colour, for instance, because our eyes are made so that when certain parts of the light spectrum 'presseth' upon our eyes, our eyes react by seeing blue. So what colours we see depends not on the object being viewed, but upon how our eyes are made. And, as we know, animals see colours differently or not at all, and many people are 'colour blind', and see different colours than the average human being. When you see green, they may see brown.

Hobbes's point here is that the information that we have about the world around us is inevitably filtered through our senses. We can know what we sense; we cannot completely know the outside world. The Aristotelian view was that the outside world communicated to us the truth about external things. The university professors who held this view taught that 'for the cause of *vision*, that the thing seen, sendeth forth on every side a *visible species*, in English, a *visible show*, *apparition*, or *aspect*, or *a being seen*; the receiving whereof into the eye, is *seeing*' (22).

What is the real difference between Hobbes's view and the Aristotelian view? After all, Hobbes believes that objects somehow make an impression upon our senses, and Aristotle believes that objects send forth a sort of message for us to intercept. The difference is not in the idea that objects somehow send us signals, but in assumptions about the content of those signals. For Hobbes, the signals are pure physical things, and so are our eyes, ears, tongues and so on. There is no inherent meaning within the signals they send, and there is no inherent meaning in how we perceive them. One man, because of his angle and because of his own physical peculiarities will hear beautiful music, another will hear an off-key din. From the Aristotelian perspective, there are certain standards inherent in nature. For instance, there is such a thing as beauty in the absolute sense; if a man hears a din when the music is objectively beautiful, there is something wrong with his judgement and he needs to work on it. Scholars who followed the Aristotelian way thought they could argue about a question such as 'what is beautiful?' and that they could eventually reach the truth of the matter. Hobbes believed such arguments were futile, and worse, even dangerous when men argued about such absolutes as 'what is just?' or 'what is moral?' or 'what constitutes good government?'

The fact that Hobbes sees human perception as purely a physical thing, and nature as purely physical as well, has much importance for the rest of his work. Nature does not have a reasonable order which can be understood by man, an order in which the law of nature or God ultimately reigns supreme and to which man can reasonably submit. This was the Aristotelian and Christian view of nature which Hobbes disagrees with from the start. All we can know is what our senses tell us, and since our senses disagree, individuals will always disagree. The project of the 'philosophy-schools' he mentions in this chapter and denigrates throughout the book – the project of discovering the truth and submitting to it – is a waste of time and an endeavour more likely to lead to continuous conflict than to agreement and peace.

Something needs to be said about Hobbes's attitude towards the universities at this point. As we know, Hobbes worked as a tutor and advisor to the Cavendish family. He was not a professor at a university. So, he was certainly criticizing them 'from the outside'. Universities such as Oxford and Cambridge before the English Civil War and change of governments were dominated by Anglican 'divines' (ministers) and lay-professors (Shapiro 1971: 72). In the aftermath of the civil war, the dissenters attempted to put their stamp on the university by removing Anglican administrators and replacing them with their own personnel who were theologically correct. After the Restoration, the Anglican leadership was put back in place. When Hobbes complains about the fuzzy theology taught at the universities, he is primarily referring to the Anglican dominance that was in place before the change in government.

It is true that the university's primary mission was to 'train clergymen and educate gentlemen' (Shapiro 1971: 72). Most people in positions of leadership were Anglican ministers (and later dissenting ministers), so that the focus of what they considered a classical education was not science, but theology and philosophy. Hobbes takes this tendency as the basis for his entire evaluation of the universities, and he conflates the way Anglican scholars philosophized with what he saw as the irrationalities and superstitions of Catholicism and Catholic philosophy (it was, after all, through Catholic theology that Aristotle came to prominence in philosophy and even in science at the universities).

Also unfair, perhaps, is his depiction of the universities as devoid of science. As Shapiro points out, there was plenty of the 'new science' being taught in universities, and neither the Anglican leadership nor the later dissenting leadership were particularly hostile to it. There were professors who lectured on the latest in mathematics, astronomy, botany and other sciences. In addition, a great deal of instruction was done through personal tutors, so that anyone who wanted to receive an up-to-date scientific education could have one. The university libraries, rather than shunning scientific texts, were collecting them, and making them available to any who wanted to benefit from them. Hobbes must have known this, but maintained a frontal assault on the universities nonetheless, his criticism no doubt consciously lacking in nuance in order to invoke the reader's disdain for traditional academics. There were others at this time railing at the universities in much the same way, including William Dell and John Webster. The latter used the memory of the great scientist Francis Bacon to sharply criticize the universities. But unlike Hobbes, the Puritans Dell and Webster were not very scientifically informed themselves, and mainly motivated by the idea of expunging superstition from the universities and keeping the Puritan clergy free of theological corruption. Shapiro points out: 'The attacks of Dell and Webster and other religious radicals, which were at a height in 1653 and again in 1659, shocked both Puritan and Anglican university men' (Shapiro 1971: 65).

Hobbes must have decided to add his voice to the chorus of criticism for his own purposes – primarily his desire to make the universities receptive to his scientific political theory. In order for this to happen, Aristotle would have to be ejected from academia – otherwise there would continue to be a discussion of just and unjust government and leadership, and the idea of popular control of government.

Hobbes continues to apply his theme of materialism to the human mind in chapter 2, 'Of Imagination'. He argues that memory and imagination are both products of our senses – the products of original sensations impressed more or less permanently on the brain. Sometimes the brain combines various memories to create compound imaginations. If we're not careful (and rational) we might think that we've come up with something entirely new through the use of our imagination, but we have really only combined that which we have already seen or known in an unusual way. Likewise, we might think that we have seen or experienced something in a dream that is prophetic or gives us a completely new idea, but Hobbes argues that dreams are really just products of physical stimuli, past and present:

> And because in sense, the brain and nerves, which are the necessary organs of sense, are so benumbed in sleep, as not easily to be moved by the action of external objects, there can happen in sleep no imagination, and therefore no dream, but what proceeds from the agitation of the inward parts of man's body; which inward parts, for the connexion they have with the brain, and other organs, when they be distempered, do keep the same in motion; whereby the imaginations there formerly made, appear as if a man were waking; saving that the organs of sense being now benumbed, so as there is no new object, which can master and obscure them with a more vigorous impression, a dream must needs be more clear, in this silence of sense, than our waking thoughts. And hence it cometh to pass, that it is a hard matter, and by many thought impossible, to distinguish exactly between sense and dreaming. (25)

What is Hobbes getting at here? We see that he thinks that memories, imaginations, and dreams are all basically the same type of thing: they are all products of decaying sense, all caused by our own senses instead of external objects. It may seem real at the time when we dream or imagine. It may seem so vivid that we think we have received some revelation that is external to us. But Hobbes is arguing against the idea that somehow a human being can have direct access to external truth, through visions, dreams, or any other means. Just as he argued against the idea of objective external truth in the first chapter, he continues the argument here, aiming with particular might against those who would claim to have 'received' some revelation or truth from inspiration or dreams. We can see his overall intent quite clearly if we read his discussion of the physical causes of dreams and imaginations in the context of the entire chapter.

Hobbes aims his arrows at those who believe in the supernatural, particularly Catholics, who were easy targets at that time in England. He conflates the belief in fairy tales with the use of holy water, for instance: 'And for fairies, and walking ghosts, the opinion of them has, I think, been on purpose either taught or not confuted, to keep in credit the use of exorcism, of crosses, of holy water, and other such inventions of ghostly men' (27). And he makes it quite clear why such beliefs are so dangerous to his political plan: 'If this superstitious fear of spirits were taken away, and with it, prognostics from dreams, false prophecies, and many other things depending thereon, by which crafty ambitious persons abuse the simple people, men would be much more fitted than they are for civil obedience' (27). He complains that the universities are teaching superstition when they should be eradicating it.

In chapter 3, which is also about imagination, Hobbes makes a special point of saying that human beings cannot truly comprehend the 'infinite'. He argues that this is a word we use when we just cannot understand something because it is too big. Another important point he makes is that man is to be distinguished from all other animals because of his ability to speak and thus to develop his intellect to a far greater degree than animals. This focus is continued in chapter 4, 'Of Speech'. In chapter 4, Hobbes seems to agree with Aristotle at first, when he says that without speech, and thus intellect, there could be no commonwealth or any human society. But he goes on to argue in a peculiar way, that speech is an 'invention' (i.e. of man). Hobbes does say that God was the 'first author of *speech*', but he goes out of his way to point out that God only directed Adam to name the animals. God did not have anything directly to do with the terms which developed: they were purely the inventions of man. Some were useful, others were not: '. . . for I do not find any thing in the Scripture, out of which, directly or by consequence, can be gathered, that Adam was taught the names of all figures, numbers, measures, colours, sounds, fancies, relations; much less the names of words and speech, as *general*, *special*, *affirmative*, *negative*, *interrogative*, *optative*, *infinitive*, all which are useful; and least of all, of *entity*, *intentionality*, *quiddity*, and other insignificant words of the school' (33).

Here Hobbes insults the universities once again, pointing out that the words they have invented are 'insignificant', that is, they make no sense. Hobbes will time and again call their language 'absurd', and this starts the theme Hobbes will fully develop on the need for precise and concrete language upon which all can agree. If words are human inventions they should serve a concrete purpose, as he says they did after God struck down the Tower of Babel and made human beings speak many languages. Languages developed more and more words out of 'need, the mother of all inventions . . .' (34). The implication is that the words used by intellectuals are not invented and do not have their origins in need but in arrogance and the desire to be obscure. But words should simply be useful tools. There needn't be any mystery surrounding them. It is in pursuit of precision, and discovering what words are useful and how they should be developed, that Hobbes proceeds into a lengthy discussion of names and naming. To make his point perfectly clear, he turns back to 'Inconstant names' at the end of chapter 4: 'The names of such things as affect us, that is, which please and displease us, because all men be not alike affected with the same thing, nor the same man at all times, are in the common discourse of men of incon-stant signification. For seeing all names are imposed to signify our conceptions, and all our affections are but conceptions, when we conceive the same things differently, we can hardly avoid different naming of them' (39–40).

In other words, value-words are inherently subjective, and thus not much use, 'for one man calleth wisdom, what another calleth fear; and one cruelty, what another justice', and so on (40). Hobbes argues that there can never be any agreement about these value-words. Academics in the universities may spend most of their time trying to define these words and arguing about whether this or that institution is just or unjust, but in doing so they are really only expressing their own personal perspectives and not a universal value. Their arguments go nowhere, or to be more precise, they are simply stirring people up to further disagreement and argument. Hobbes is going to show that 'Reason and Science' (the title of chapter 5) stand in opposition to the fuzzy philosophy at the universities, which is all too often applied to the most important of subjects: the order of the commonwealth.

In chapter 5, Hobbes reveals the ideal way to build a political philosophy. He defines reason as a 'mathematical' activity: the adding and subtracting of concepts and names, a process he calls 'reckoning'. He tells us that we should not simply trust old and respected authors for our information. We should reason for ourselves, starting from the logical beginning and working forward. Or, if we cannot reason for ourselves in this way, we should insist on having the truth of things demonstrated for us. Academics developed absurd words and arguments because they did not start with good definitions, and thus they could not demonstrate what they were saying. Hobbes points out that the method of arguing strictly from definitions, which do not shift and change to suit the arguer, is only practised in the science of geometry. His intention is to create the only true science of politics by creating a verbal geometric method by which to reason about political things. The beauty of this method is that, unlike the inconstant and absurd names and reasoning of academics, a doctrine built upon useful and clear definitions can be understood by everyone. In an epiphany which should stand as a precursor to Enlightenment thought, Hobbes proclaims, 'the light of human minds is perspicuous words, but by exact definitions first snuffed, and purged from ambiguity; reason is the pace; increase of science, the way; and the benefit of mankind, the end. And, on the contrary, metaphors, and senseless and ambiguous words, are like *ignes fatui*; and reasoning upon them is wandering amongst innumerable absurdities; and their end, contention and sedition, or contempt' (45–46).

In pursuit of verbal accuracy and precision, Hobbes spends a great deal of time in this chapter tearing apart some of the words of academics, which he thinks are nonsense, such as '*hypostatical, transubstantiate, consubstantiate, eternal-now . . .*' (44).[1]

'Transubstantiate' is the word Catholics use to describe the transformation the Eucharist makes from bread and wine to the Body and Blood of Christ. Similarly, 'consubstantiate' refers to the doctrine of the Lutherans that Christ's presence commingles with the bread and wine. Hobbes's general rule is that if you cannot see it, there is no reason to believe it is there. If the words make no literal sense, then they should not be used.

Next, Hobbes turns to what he believes is the great problem in human nature – the passions. Chapter 6 is 'Of the Interior Beginnings of Voluntary Motions; Commonly called the Passions; and the Speeches by which they are expressed'. He begins by proclaiming that all passions come from either 'appetite' (desire or attraction) or 'aversion' (being repelled by something). He argues again that people call whatever they desire good and whatever repels them bad, and that there is no common agreement on what is attractive or repulsive, good or bad. Certainly, there is no absolute or common rule that can be taken from the nature of objects themselves – value judgements are truly subjective. Hobbes goes on to attempt to define some of the words that signify passions, such as hope, despair, fear and courage. By doing so he does not end the argument he describes, because, as he has pointed out, each person applies these words to different objects.

Deliberation, according to Hobbes, is the process of the back-and-forth motions of our passions:

> When in the mind of man, appetites, and aversions, hopes, and fears, concerning one and the same thing, arise alternately; and divers good and evil consequences of the doing, or omitting the thing propounded, come successively into our thoughts; so that sometimes we have an appetite to it; sometimes an aversion from it; sometimes hope to be able to do it; sometimes despair, or fear to attempt it; the whole sum of desires, aversions, hopes and fears continued till the thing be done, or thought impossible, is that we call DELIBERATION. (53)

Remember that everything that human beings think and feel originally comes from physical causes, from the reaction of their senses to what is around them in the world. So it is with the passions; they are affected by our own physical internal make-up. Hobbes is claiming that when we deliberate, when we think through what we want to do, it is our passions that are mostly involved, not our reason. He tells us that will is the '*last appetite in deliberating*' (54): our willing is nothing more than the expression of our last appetite. Since it is the product of a chain of physical causes, Hobbes leaves us to wonder whether or not man really has free will, and indeed Hobbes often argues in *Leviathan* and elsewhere that human beings really do not have free will; yet at other times through the very assumptions and structure of his argument, he seems to assume free will – if people do not have free choice, why would he even attempt to persuade his readers to think and act differently?

Next, Hobbes argues in chapter 7 that there can be no absolute knowledge even in science because original sensory things are thought about using our memory. If that is so, all knowledge is conditional. What makes knowledge a product of science is the process through which the knowledge has been gained. If discourse starts with definitions and moves logically to generalizations, syllogisms, and conclusions, it is science. If it does not, it should be called opinion. Hobbes makes an effort to break down the idea of 'conscience', which people often use to stick stubbornly to their opinions and refuse to submit to a greater power. He explains that when two or more people agree on a fact, we say that they are 'conscious' of that fact. To ask a person to deny such a fact would 'be reputed a very evil act'. That, he says, would be asking a man to 'speak against his *conscience*. . .' (57). Notice how he is defining conscience as being conscious of the same fact along with other people – not the usual definition. Then, Hobbes makes his point:

> Afterwards, men made use of the same word metaphorically, for the knowledge of their own secret facts, and secret thoughts; and therefore it is rhetorically said, that the conscience is a thousand witnesses. And last of all, men, vehemently in love with their own new opinions, though never so absurd, and obstinately bent to maintain them, gave those their opinions also that reverenced name of conscience, as if they would have it seem unlawful, to change or speak against them; and so pretend to know they are true, when they know at most, but that they think so. (57)

Hobbes has thus redefined 'conscience' so that those people who claim to disobey the law because of their moral scruples are wrong and are simply asserting their own ignorant and egotistical opinions. Definitions do indeed matter!

Chapter 8 can be seen as an attempt to define intellectual virtue, but if so, the reader might miss the larger point. Hobbes wants to talk about why people are not more rational, why so often they make mistakes, or have intellectual 'defects' that lead to, among other things, madness and superstition. As we have seen already, man is more of a passionate than a rational animal. Passions are caused both by our physical state and also by our experiences and education. The fact that our passions most often direct our thinking, decisions, and actions is simply a fact of life which leads to a universal truth of sorts. This truth becomes a centerpiece of Hobbes's political philosophy: all men ultimately desire power. 'The passions that most of all cause the difference of wit, are principally, the more or less desire of power, of riches, of knowledge, and of honour. All which may be reduced to the first, that is, desire of power. For riches, knowledge, and honour, are but several sorts of power' (62).

Hobbes assumes that this desire for power will influence men's actions in the state of nature. If all men are by nature passionate, and those passions conflict, and if all passions or desires for things are expressed by a lust for power in order to get them, then men not under the control of a dominant government of some kind will be in constant conflagration. This is exactly the situation he discusses in Part II of *Leviathan*. The rest of chapter 8, though, deals with madness and 'giddiness' which are excesses of passion. This at least indicates that passions can be under some self-control (since not everyone is insane). Hobbes says at one point that 'unguided' passions are madness, which implies that we can, after all, somewhat guide our passions. If that is true, then the picture is not totally hopeless. If we were merely creatures of our passions, we could not hope to escape them through any logical theory, even Hobbes.

Further, Hobbes addresses the issue of madness in relation to the Bible's treatment of demonic possession. While he does not declare that there are no such things as demons, Hobbes gives a good example of his ability to reinterpret scripture from a modern scientific perspective when he asks the question, 'But why then does our Saviour proceed in the curing of them, as if they were possessed; and not as if they were mad?' (66-7). He compares those who argue that this demonic possession was real with those who argue that the Bible tells us the sun orbits the earth. This type of information is not the main purpose of the Bible, argues Hobbes, and to make clear his way of reading the Bible, he explains: 'As for that our Saviour speaketh to the disease as to a person; it is the usual phrase of all that cure by words only, as Christ did, and enchanters pretend to do, wither they speak to a devil or not. For is Christ also said (*Matt.* viii. 26) to have rebuked the winds? Is not he said also (*Luke* iv. 39) to rebuke a fever? Yet this does not argue that a fever is a devil. And whereas many of the devils are said to confess Christ; it is not necessary to interpret those places otherwise, than that those madmen confessed him' (67).

Hobbes is certainly rationalizing the Bible. When you read his interpretation of biblical passages you should be aware of his methods and intentions. First, he is not a literalist. This is made clear by the passage above. The Bible literally refers to demons, but Hobbes argues that this reference to demons is supposed to be taken *figuratively* for mental illness. Second, his aim is always to demystify the Bible – to make its contents somehow in accord with scientific fact, naturally occurring phenomena, or as a last resort, psychological illusion. Finally, Hobbes is always striving to make sure that the Bible does not contradict his view of human nature and, more importantly, his argument for the desirability of absolute earthly rule.

In chapter 9, Hobbes gives us a neat definition of science. It is conditional knowledge, '*knowledge of the consequence of one affirmation to another*' (69). That is, it is not a set of facts but a type of knowledge that proceeds logically from predetermined definitions. It is not absolute knowledge, because as we found out earlier, there can be no absolute knowledge: we only have the impressions of our senses, which may be false. If new facts and information appear to us, then we must be willing to start with different definitions. Hobbes provides us with a handy flow chart of types of science. He distinguishes between natural philosophy and civil philosophy. Natural philosophy treats natural bodies, but civil philosophy deals with what he has earlier called 'artificial bodies' and here calls '*politic* bodies'. There are only two branches jutting from this latter category of civil philosophy: the rights and duties of the sovereign and the duty and right (notice the difference in order and plurals) of the subjects (70).

Chapter 10 is interesting because it indicates how during Hobbes's time, everything was being questioned. The old-fashioned notions of what it meant to be a gentleman, to be honourable and chivalrous, were being whittled away. Nowhere is this more apparent than in Hobbes's reinterpretation of honour in this chapter. He starts out defining power: '*Power*. The power *of a man*, to take it universally, is his present means, to obtain some future apparent good; and is either *original* or *instrumental*' (72). He then discusses the difference between the powers given to us by nature, such as our physical strength, and our strength of mind, and those that are acquired, such as riches and friends. But the truly interesting thing about this chapter is that Hobbes consistently undermines the old-fashioned notions of honour and worthiness. From the older aristocratic point of view, a man was honourable because of his moral qualities, at least as an ideal. He was worthy because of the type of man he was: his quality, his character, his courage, and so on. But Hobbes reduces honour and worthiness to power.

First, he argues that all the things that people admire as honourable are forms of power, because all tend to cause others to do what we want. For instance, he writes that 'what quality soever maketh a man beloved, or feared of many; or the reputation of such quality, is power; because it is a means to have the assistance, and service of many' (72). So far, though his focus is definitely on power, one could still attribute the older moral force to this idea of reputation as power. But Hobbes goes on to define honourable and dishonourable:

> *Honourable. Honourable* is whatsovever possession, action, or quality, is an argument and sign of power.
>    *Dishonourable*. And therefore to be honoured, loved, or feared of many, is honourable; as arguments of power. To be honoured of few or none, *dishonourable*. (75)

Either Hobbes is guilty of circular reasoning here, or he is saying that honour is really just another word for power. Whoever has power will also be esteemed honourable and worthy. Hobbes is not usually guilty of making circular arguments; he tries to be painstakingly logical. Further proof that Hobbes is simply reducing honour to power is found in his list of classical virtues, all of which he reduces in the same way: 'Magnanimity, liberality, hope, courage, confidence, are honourable, for they proceed from the conscience of power. Pusilanimity, parsimony, fear, diffidence, are dishonourable' (75). In other words, we see these virtues as honourable because they belong to a person who is powerful. They are indications of power. Likewise, the following vices are usually signs that a person does not have power and knows it. And just to be perfectly clear on this point, Hobbes openly deals with the question of whether moral considerations come into play at all when deciding whether someone or something is honourable: 'Nor does it alter the case of honour, whether an action so it be great and difficult, and consequently a sign of much power, be just or unjust; for honour consisteth only in the opinion of power' (76).

At the end of this chapter, Hobbes deals with typical symbols of honour in the nobility, such as coats of arms and titles. He points out that these are only considered to be honourable if the sovereign makes them so. He also points out that a man's worthiness or fitness for something is quite different from his worth. To be worthy is to have a particular aptitude for something. The worth of a man, as Hobbes says earlier in this chapter, is simply 'his price' – 'so much as would be given for the use of his power . . .' (73). Whether or not a man is worthy or particularly fit to perform a particular task (such as leadership) does not mean that he should do so. Again, power determines who will fulfil certain roles, not the quality of a man. This line of argument consciously contradicts the position of Plato and Aristotle that those who are best suited by aptitude to rule should be the rulers. At every turn, Hobbes is trying to close up opportunities for people to argue that their leaders are unjust and therefore should be rejected and replaced.

Hobbes further refines his description of human nature in this very famous passage in chapter 11. First he argues, 'For there is no such *finis ultimus*, utmost aim, nor *summum bonum*, greatest good, as is spoken of in the books of the old moral philosophers. Nor can a man any more live, whose desires are at an end, than he, whose senses and imaginations are at a stand. Felicity [happiness] is a continual progress of the desire, from one object to another; the attaining of the former, being still but the way to the latter' (80).

Here Hobbes is directly and openly attacking the Platonic and Aristotelian idea of the good life. He is saying that there is no agreement on what the good life is, contrary to what they argued (that the good life is the life of philosophy, the life of justice). Instead, every individual determines what is good for himself. Happiness, which the ancients argued could only be obtained by living justly, is actually just the feeling people get as they acquire what they desire. Unlike the ancients, who thought that experiencing continual desire was slavery to our passions, the modern philosopher Hobbes argues that life itself is the feeling of desires. If that feeling should cease, life itself would cease. Thus Hobbes continues:

> So that in the first place, I put for a general inclination of all mankind, a perpetual and restless desire of power after power, that ceaseth only in death. And the cause of this, is not always that a man hopes for a more intensive delight, than he has already attained to; or that he cannot be content with a moderate power: but because he cannot assure the power and means to live well, which he hath present, without the acquisition of more. (81)

If this is true, man can never really rest and simply enjoy what he has. Being content in this sense is a form of death, which could actually lead to one's physical destruction because others may take advantage and move in to take away what a man has acquired. So it

27

seems that not only is continual pursuit and obtaining of desires the essence of happiness, but it is also the logical means of security and survival.

Hobbes then goes on to discuss which aspects of human nature tend to produce conflict and which encourage people to obey a common power. Love of competition causes conflict, but desire to live an easy life of pleasure leads people to obey. Interestingly, here Hobbes places fear of death second in his list of what leads men to desire a 'common power'. Hobbes delves deeper into human nature, and the picture is not very pretty. Feeling a sense of obligation to another, for instance, causes people to be outwardly grateful, but inwardly resentful. This is an ugly thought, but it is difficult to disagree totally with Hobbes's view.

Here Hobbes also begins his frequent criticism of 'vain-glorious men' – those who are arrogant and ambitious, those who take no risks themselves, but rather use other people whom they flatter and provoke to do their bidding. 'Vain-glorious men' were the chief cause, in his view, of the English Civil War. Rebellious Dissenting ministers and other figures, hoping to empower themselves, used inflammatory rhetoric to anger the people into supporting open revolt against the monarch. On the other side, Hobbes blames ignorance of natural causes (a lack of familiarity with science) and lack of understanding in general for the gullibility of the people.

Hobbes develops the theme of religion in the next chapter (chapter 12, 'Of Religion'). He starts out arguing that the 'seed of religion' is in man. What he means is that only human beings reason enough to inquire into the cause of things, and so the idea of God occurs to them, but not to other creatures. He then expands on his argument about curiosity and natural religion which he actually began at the end of the previous chapter. Finally, he makes this statement, in some ways worthy of Karl Marx:

> *The natural cause of religion, the anxiety of the time to come.* The two first [the desire to know causes and the consideration of the beginning of things], make anxiety. For being assured that there be causes of all things that have arrived hitherto, or shall arrive hereafter; it is impossible for a man, who continually endeavoureth to secure himself against the evil he fears, and procure the good he desireth, not to be in a perpetual solicitude of the time to come; so that every man, especially those that are over provident, are in a state like to that of Prometheus. (87)

Hobbes is referring to the natural tendency in man, the curious creature, to wonder about not only the causes of things but also his own future. In particular, man is the only creature who knows that he will die, and this produces fear and anxiety. Of course such a creature will wonder what happens after death, and this fear and wonder cause what Hobbes calls natural religion, human thoughts about creation and the Creator. Hobbes describes this human situation as Promethean.[2] In Greek mythology Prometheus was the god who felt sorry for human beings and so gave them the gift of fire. As a punishment for empowering people, Zeus had Prometheus chained to a rock, where a vulture pecked out his liver by day and it was miraculously healed every night. Hobbes interprets the myth by saying that Prometheus represents 'the prudent man'. And Hobbes completes the analogy by observing that man has 'his heart all the day long, gnawed on by fear of death, poverty, or other calamity; and has no repose, nor pause of his anxiety, but in sleep' (88). It is fear and anxiety which produces fear of '*the power of invisible things*' (88).

Chapter 13 is one of the most important and famous chapters in *Leviathan*. In it, Hobbes describes 'the natural condition of mankind', his 'state of nature'. Upon this description he builds much of the rest of his political philosophy. Hobbes does not think that mankind is naturally sociable or good, but is rather naturally individualistic and selfish. When he imagines what human beings would be like without government, he does not paint a pretty picture. And yet, man's natural condition without government establishes certain principles and fundamental rights upon which Hobbes believes he can build a lasting and stable political order. One of the principles emerging from Hobbes's state of nature is the natural equality of all people. This may be hard to understand at first, because it would seem that especially in nature, inequalities of strength and stamina would be crucial. But Hobbes reasons that each is equally a threat to every other in nature – enough of a threat to warrant all to fear all when there is no power of government to restrain them. Even the weakest can kill the strongest when no one is watching and when the enemy's guard is down. Out of this fundamental equality comes distrust and natural competition. If everyone is a potential threat to my life, and I cannot know what is on the mind of my fellow human beings, I must act to pre-empt any violence against me before it happens. This is logical for everyone, given the situation of radical insecurity caused by anarchy, or the lack of any overarching power to subdue people. Unfortunately, this logical reaction leads to more mistrust and violence, creating a vicious cycle.

Hobbes makes it clear that some in nature will want more than others. But precisely because these ambitious people are evidence of a continual threat to the safety and security of all others, all people must model themselves on the most ambitious in order to survive. Clearly he does not think that anyone should be blamed for acting in this way. Indeed, all *ought* to act this way, because it is the only reasonable way to survive. Hobbes indicates that there are a lot of people for whom obtaining dominion is also a pleasure, and this adds to their incentive to take as much as they can and deprive others of whatever they have. Hobbes thus finds three causes of conflict among people: 'First, Competition; secondly, diffidence; thirdly, glory.' 'The first, maketh men invade for gain; the second, for safety; and the third, for reputation' (99). So we see that self-interest and fear are paramount in people's minds in the state of nature. But also, another cause of conflict is 'reputation'. Hobbes also uses words like 'pride', 'honour', and most significantly 'vainglory' to describe the same thing. This means that even in the state of nature, people will fight not only for survival and dominance but also over an insult, or just the desire to make someone else recognize their superiority. Hobbes does not think this is a desirable trait in human nature, but he must think it is nonetheless very important. It turns out to be the chief obstacle to agreement and thus peace.

Hobbes has been criticized by Rousseau among others for bringing a quintessentially social attitude – desire for glory, or pride – into his natural condition, a condition that was supposed to be pre-social. But if we think of Hobbes's state of nature not as some picture of a long-ago real situation but rather as a picture of what people in Hobbes's time would do if they were not restrained, Hobbes's depiction makes more sense. After all, it was the problems of society that Hobbes was concerned about, not those of pre-social human beings. Hobbes wanted his society to avoid civil war, in which people did become vicious with each other because of (at least in his view) their sense of pride. Hobbes's quest is largely to convince people of the need to eliminate pride and to give government the means to make pride less of a force in society. He mentions the situation of tribal people in America, and also the relations sovereign kings have with one another, as examples that come close to what he is talking about. But above all he has the English Civil War in mind, and he wants the English people to see how inimical to peace some of their attitudes are, to see that peace is more important than the principles over which it is broken. For Hobbes, life is more important than the protection of particular principles. If you lose your life, you lose the ability to pursue any other good. Hobbes seeks to remind people of this fact through his rather frightening depiction of the state of nature.

The result of the natural condition of mankind is that all human beings in this condition are of necessity in a constant state of war with all others. The by-product of this highly insecure atmosphere is misery, and Hobbes describes the life of people in the state of nature in perhaps his most memorable lines:

> In such condition, there is no place for industry; because the fruit thereof is uncertain: and consequently no culture of the earth; no navigation, nor use of the commodities that may be imported by sea; no commodious building; no instruments of moving, and removing, such things as require much force; no knowledge of the face of the earth; no account of time; no arts; no letters; no society; and which is worst of all, continual fear, and danger of violent death; and the life of man, solitary, poor, nasty, brutish and short. (100)

Notice that Hobbes gives us a very positive vision of society at peace here. It is possible for a people, once it has achieved peace, to build up an advanced civilization that can make people very happy. This is what Hobbes wants rather than constant conflict. While we might not always like Hobbes's cynical view of human nature or his negativity regarding the possibilities for real understanding, this vision helps us feel better about his intentions. All of these are things we consider good. Hobbes is calling for people to think about these things rather than their pride before they take up the sword and ruin their chances for the pleasures society can bring. He makes one more point in this chapter which ties what he has said already about the nature of values as matters of perspective to what he has also said about the state of nature:

> To this war of every man, against every man, this also is consequent; that nothing can be unjust. The notions of right and wrong, justice and

31

injustice have there no place. Where there is no common power, there is no law: where no law, no injustice. Force, and fraud, are in war the two cardinal virtues. Justice, and injustice are none of the faculties neither of the body, nor mind. If they were, they might be in a man that were alone in the world, as well as his senses, and passions. They are qualities, that relate to men in society, not in solitude. (101)

So here Hobbes makes it clear that before the social contract takes place and people put themselves under an authority other than themselves, justice and injustice simply do not exist. Indeed, what we think of as injustice is actually a virtue in warfare. Right and wrong, justice and injustice, really only appear once people make that social contract and enter into society. This is very important because Hobbes is saying here that there is no such thing as natural rights such as John Locke or the American Founders would claim. The only right that man has in nature, as we will see, is self-preservation. Any other right can only be established in society. In society, the sovereign power alone can define what is right or wrong, through the laws it creates, and the definitions of these can change according to its pleasure. We call the position Hobbes takes here 'legal positivism', which simply means that Hobbes thinks there is no just or unjust, apart from whatever the laws in a particular place dictate. There can be no appeal to a 'higher law' or 'natural law'. Hobbes needs to make this very clear, because he thinks that the appeal to higher or natural laws is precisely the fuel that feeds the flames of civil war.

Chapter 14 discusses the difference between the right of nature and laws of nature as he uniquely defines them. We will have to see how his discussion here goes along with what was said above. First, Hobbes defines the right of nature: the liberty to do whatever it takes for self-preservation. This is simply to say that when someone finds himself in the state of nature, he can do whatever he thinks necessary to save his life. In the state of nature, everyone has a right to everything they think useful to that end. A law of nature, on the other hand, is a rule discovered by reason that *prohibits* whatever is destructive to self-preservation. For Hobbes there is only one right of nature, but there are numerous laws of nature, because there are numerous behaviours and even attitudes which reason tells us to avoid if we want to live in peace. The first two laws of nature are essential for understanding the role of the rest of the laws he discusses in chapter 15. The first law of nature, he says, is to seek peace, but also to defend ourselves by any means possible. The second law of nature is to lay down our own right to all things, and to allow all other men as much liberty as we would allow ourselves: 'From this fundamental law of nature, by which men are commanded to endeavour peace, is derived this second law; that a man be willing, when others are so too, as far-forth, as for peace, and defence of himself he shall think it necessary, to lay down his right to all things; and be contented with so much liberty against other men, as he would allow other men against himself' (104).

So, while a person can never give up the right to self-preservation, under certain conditions he can give up the right to other things. These conditions involve entering into a contract.[3] Hobbes makes it clear that contracts made in nature are not binding and will not work because there is no power to enforce them. This fundamental social contract is necessary to create the circumstances of peace, so that other contracts and agreements can be binding on people. Through a contract with all others, people can give up the right to the means of self-defence to the sovereign power they create. Only after this contract has been made can there be such a thing as injustice. Injustice is the breaking of contracts, even if those contracts have been made out of fear, because even these have been made voluntarily and for a good reason – the saving of life. Thus, as we will see, Hobbes believes that it is wrong to break the social contract so long as the sovereign power is still protecting people's lives, no matter how tyrannical that sovereign is otherwise.

The rest of Hobbes's discussion of contracts, covenants and gifts in this chapter must be understood in light of what has been said above: no agreement is binding unless that fundamental agreement, the social contract, has been made. He makes this clear later on in the chapter when he writes:

If a covenant be made, wherein neither of the parties perform presently, but trust one another; in the condition of mere nature, which is a condition of war of every man against every man, upon any reasonable suspicion, it is void: but if there be a common power set over them both, with right and force sufficient to compel performance, it is not void. For he that performeth first, has no assurance the other will perform after; because the bonds of words are too weak to bridle men's ambition, avarice, anger, and other passions, without the fear of some coercive

33

power; which in the condition of mere nature, where all men are equal, and judges of the justness of their own fears, cannot possibly be supposed. (105)

Hobbes has now set the stage for introducing his other laws of nature in chapter 15. The next law of nature he discusses, the third, follows from what he has just said in the previous chapter. It is for men to 'perform their covenants made', which for Hobbes is the same as justice and propriety (ownership). He makes it clear again that justice, propriety and injustice can only exist once the social contract is made, when other contracts become enforceable. This is the very meaning and purpose of the commonwealth or political community for Hobbes, the establishment of a sovereign power that can enforce the law and thus allow people within reason to trust each other, make agreements, and build up what they own.

Before he moves on to the fourth and all the other laws of nature, Hobbes pauses to argue with a fool. Under the subheading, 'Justice not contrary to reason', Hobbes says, 'The fool hath said in his heart, that there is no such thing as justice. . .' (114). Hobbes wants to combat those who would argue that it is reasonable sometimes to break contracts and be deceitful *even once in civil society*, if you can get away with it. He characterizes such people harshly, saying that they think it may sometimes be reasonable to be unjust, 'taking away the fear of God, for the same fool hath said in his heart there is no God . . .' (114).[4] This is rather strong language from Hobbes, and what comes next, which also involves God, is hard to understand, and so we need to examine it closely:

> The kingdom of God is gotten by violence: but what if it could be gotten by unjust violence? were it against reason to so get it, when it is impossible to receive hurt by it? and if it be not against reason, it is not against justice; or else justice is not to be approved for good. From such reasoning as this, successful wickedness hath obtained the name of virtue: and some that in all other things have disallowed the violation of faith; yet have allowed it, when it is for the getting of a kingdom. (114)

Here, Hobbes is writing using another's voice, in this case the voice of the fool he has described above, without telling the reader that he is doing so. If we read the beginning of this quotation as being said or thought by the fool, and if we remember the historical context of

Hobbes, we can begin to see that he is really characterizing the thought process of someone whom Hobbes might call a religious zealot, someone willing to do what most of the time would be considered unjust, but who thinks that the ends justify the means (Hoekstra 1997). If such a person believes they can obtain heaven, either personally or for their community, by committing an injustice such as breaching the social contract and deposing the sovereign, then they will think that whatever they do to obtain that ultimate good must be just. But Hobbes comments that it is precisely this kind of self-justifying reasoning that has been responsible for much wickedness in the world, and especially the wickedness which he has just seen in his own country with the demise of Charles I. He calls such reasoning 'specious' or false, as if calling it the reasoning of a fool was not clear enough.

Hobbes reminds his readers again of the misery that can come from a state of war, where everyone thinks as the fool thinks and no one is there to restrain them from creating a world of total conflict. As for the goal of getting to heaven, this goal, in his view, cannot be obtained by those who break covenants. In fact, he says, the only way to obtain the 'felicity of heaven' is 'not breaking, but keeping of covenant' (115). Since there is no natural knowledge of what happens to people after death, Hobbes does not believe any arguments about obtaining heaven by this or that action can be reasonable. In other words, he strongly questions those who would say they know how to get to heaven, especially those who urge war in order to get there. Hobbes goes on to identify the man who keeps his covenants, and rejects the temptation to gain what he wants by breaching his promises, as having 'a certain nobleness or gallantness of courage, rarely found . . .' (116–117). In this way, Hobbes appeals to men's pride for positive reinforcement of his ideas, whereas he usually thinks of pride as destructive. Perhaps if pride can be connected with Hobbes's priorities it can become an acceptable form of motivation.

The rest of chapter 15 goes on to list and define the other laws of nature, such as 'facility to pardon', or 'against contumely' (hatred or contempt). As you read these laws, remember that they cannot be made binding on the sovereign, and so they cannot be used to criticize the sovereign. Nevertheless, they are rational rules that are sensible to follow once people are in a setting of civil society in which they can feel safe. Hobbes details them here as guidance to both rulers and those they govern in dealing with their fellow human beings in a peaceful and orderly way. '*The science of these laws is the true moral philosophy*', Hobbes writes (123). Even though he himself has called them the laws of nature, at the end of this chapter, Hobbes reminds us that only those laws that are put in place and enforced by a sovereign power are real laws. If not, then they are merely 'conclusions' or 'theorems concerning what conduceth to the conservation and defence' of human beings. Hobbes gives a nod to biblical authority, however, adding that if these theorems are given to us in the 'word of God' then we can call them laws (124). We are left to wonder exactly how this could be so, if true laws must be promulgated and enforced by an earthly power.

The final chapter in Part I is entitled 'Of Persons, Authors, and Things Personated'. Here Hobbes explains how the sovereign is created by the social contract and how we are to view the sovereign once created. Right away, he introduces the idea of an 'artificial person' who represents the words and actions of others. Your edition of *Leviathan* may have the original picture of a king, whose body, if you look closely, is made up of many other people. This picture gives us a visual image of what Hobbes means. Through the social contract the people are united in this artificial person in order to accomplish the tasks of the state.

Remember that in the social contract the people give up all their rights (except the fundamental right of self-preservation) to the sovereign, who then acts as their representative. To use Hobbes's language here, the sovereign 'personates' them. The people who created the sovereign Hobbes calls 'the author', whereas the sovereign is the 'actor'. Once power has been given to the actor, all his actions must be seen as those of the author, the people. It is not permissible for them to disagree with the sovereign's actions because they, ultimately, are the authors of all his actions, having once given up their rights to him in the social contract. Only if the people limit the sovereign actor's representation in some way would this not be so. While Hobbes repeatedly offers this idea of limited sovereignty or limited representation as a possible outcome of the social contract, and even the possibility that the artificial person might not be one man but an assembly with majority rule, we will see that he thinks such outcomes to be impossible and even absurd in practice. The argument for rule by one as superior to rule by a few (aristocracy) or by many (democracy) will appear, among many other arguments, in Part II of *Leviathan*.

## Questions

1. How does Hobbes's treatment of the human body, especially of sense perception, shape his opinions on human nature? Does it help explain why people so often find themselves in disagreement or conflict with each other?
2. How does Hobbes deal with phenomena such as dreams, visions, imagination, and religious ideas such as transubstantiation and demonic possession? What was his purpose in casting doubt on the prevailing views of these phenomena?
3. What is the 'natural condition of mankind' and how does Hobbes use this idea to explain to his readers why they need a strong government?
4. How does Hobbes want us to view the laws of nature? Are they binding in the state of nature? If not, what role do they play?

## PART II: OF COMMONWEALTH

Part II has long been considered the most important part of *Leviathan* because it contains Hobbes's full vision of how and why the commonwealth is created. But Hobbes himself reminds us of the importance of his discussion of human nature in Part I by recalling his dire vision of the state of nature in order to say, at the beginning of Part II, that the goal of the commonwealth must be security or self-preservation. The laws of nature and covenants among men, he repeats, have no reality without a common power, the 'sword', to enforce them. Next, Hobbes turns to confront Aristotle's idea that man is a social animal, like the bees or ants. Hobbes will argue against those who think that people do not need an absolute government to keep the peace. He asks the question, if animals that do not even speak can find a way to cooperate with one another and therefore could be called by Aristotle 'political creatures', then why cannot human beings cooperate for the common good in the same way? Of course, Aristotle thought they could, if they were given the proper government to guide their behaviour. He thought that human beings' social nature could be channelled into good citizenship, that responsibility for the common good could indeed be fostered under certain circumstances, and thus he did not advocate an absolute monarchy. Hobbes uses six arguments to refute Aristotle's view of mankind's sociability. All of these arguments point to an area of human nature that Hobbes believes even the social animals do not share: pride.

Hobbes points out that human beings compete all the time for honour, but animals do not. While the biologist might not agree after observing primate and other animal behaviour, this statement simply points up that, for Hobbes, pride is the greatest reason for human conflict. In his view, human beings are not so much a-social as anti-social. Next, Hobbes argues that for social creatures, the private interest and the common interest are the same – each ant does its job by instinct, because of the need to eat, procreate, and so on. But human beings often see their individual interest as very distinct, indeed opposed to, the common interest. Hobbes then takes a swipe at the people in his own society who were, in his view, causing so many problems. 'Thirdly, that these creatures, having not, as man, the use of reason, do not see, nor think they see any fault, in the administration of their common business; whereas amongst men, there are very many, that think themselves wiser, and abler to govern the public, better than the rest; and these strive to reform and innovate, one this way, another that way; and thereby bring it into distraction and civil war' (131).

Notice that it is reason that gets people into so much trouble. What Aristotle thought would help human beings to better govern themselves is seen by Hobbes as so tangled up with human pride that it does not guide people to peace but to war. Bees, in other words, do not think enough to criticize their 'government', but every person has enough reason to do so. Further, every person believes he has superior wisdom, so he second-guesses and criticizes those in power. From this position of pride comes the idea of reform or revolution.

In Hobbes's fourth point, human speech is seen as causing more harm than good. For Aristotle, the fact that human beings could use complex speech meant that they could use it to deliberate with each other for the common good. But Hobbes argues here that this gift of speech is much more likely to be used to bash political enemies, lie to people about what is good for them, and stir up disobedience. Fifthly, Hobbes points out that animals are not 'offended' unless they are truly hurt by others. But human beings can feel offended even if their fellow human beings have done nothing that directly hurts them (for instance, by ignoring them). Hobbes's last point bears repeating because it reminds his readers of what he has already said about the social contract in Part I and places it in the context of his argument with Aristotle. 'Lastly, the agreement of these creatures is natural; that of men, is by covenant only, which is artificial; and therefore it is no wonder if there be somewhat else required, besides covenant, to make their agreement constant and lasting; which is a common power, to keep them in awe, and to direct their actions to the common benefit' (131–2).

Hobbes simply disagrees with Aristotle that human beings are inclined to society and peace, and he disagrees that political communities arise naturally. For Aristotle the first political community is the family, with the father as head. This community naturally expands into the village, and then the city. At the level of the city, fatherly authority is not good enough, and more people have to be involved in governance. But Aristotle depicts each type of governance as natural and, at some level, based upon consent and common agreement for the common good – even the rule of the father over his family. As we will see, Hobbes would even dispute that the nuclear family is natural, let alone the political community (indeed, even in this chapter he refers to a man making his children submit to his authority through force).

Hobbes thinks human beings see themselves as individuals first and foremost. Their self-interest will always come first, even if it is directly at the expense of others. If this is so, then the only way to keep the peace among people would be to impose order through a government with absolute power. There can be no direct participation by the citizens in their governance without the risk of civil conflict. Though Aristotle definitely understood the risk of civil conflict, he believed that the truly human life was the public life, the life of the citizen involved in the affairs of his community. Aristotle was not willing to accept the life of total submission in order to obtain peace.

Hobbes emphasizes that the artificial person is created when each person agrees with every other person to give up their rights to self-government either to one man or to an assembly of men, and to authorize all the sovereign's subsequent actions. 'This is the generation of that great LEVIATHAN, or rather, to speak more reverently, of that *mortal god*, to which we owe under the *immortal God*, our peace and defence' (132). This is striking language indeed, to call the government both a leviathan and a mortal god. You will recall that the leviathan appears in the book of Job, and that it is a creature which God uses to demonstrate his vast power. Here

Hobbes makes the leviathan human government, and thus connects godlike power with the power of the commonwealth. It is not clear whether by 'under the immortal God' he means that the government is under God, or whether we owe government obedience because God wills it. Later we will see that the second interpretation is the more likely. Hobbes will argue that God has left the governing of people to their earthly sovereigns, at least for the time being.

Hobbes spends chapter 18 discussing the rights sovereigns have once they are created. As we might imagine, these rights are extensive. Most important, he points out at the very beginning that once the people have made a covenant to create the sovereign, they cannot break that covenant.[5] To do so under any circumstances would be unjust. In chapter 19, he turns to defending monarchy over any other type of government, and his argument is worth looking at in detail in order to understand why Hobbes is so convinced that other types of government would be disastrous.

In the first part of chapter 19, Hobbes picks a fight with the ancients once again, proclaiming that there are only three types of government: monarchy, aristocracy, and democracy (the rule of the one, the few, or the many). Plato and Aristotle thought that there were more forms of government than these three: monarchy (rule by one who is wise), tyranny (arbitrary and selfish rule by one), timocracy (military rule), aristocracy (rule by the few wise), oligarchy (rule by the rich), democracy (law-abiding rule by the many), and anarchy (lawless rule by the many). Aristotle also proposed a new mixed form of government called polity, a government that would be stronger than any of these unmixed forms by forcing parts of society to work together and compromise (namely the common majority and the wealthy few). Hobbes rejects all of these forms of government, though he does not address the polity in this chapter:

> There by other names of government, in the histories, and books of policy; as *tyranny*, and *oligarchy*: but they are not the names of other forms of government, but of the same forms misliked. For they that are discontented under *monarchy*, call it *tyranny*; and they that are displeased with *aristocracy*, call it *oligarchy*: so also, they which find themselves grieved under a *democracy*, call it *anarchy*, which signifies want of government; and yet I think no man believes, that want of government, is any new kind of government: nor by the same reason ought they to

believe, that the government is of one kind, when they like it, and another, when they mislike it, or are oppressed by the governors. (142)

So whereas the ancients thought that tyranny, oligarchy, and anarchy were different forms of government, partly because the intentions and quality of the rulers in them were different, and partly because these forms functioned differently in practice, Hobbes believes that they are simply different terms for monarchy, aristocracy, and democracy. You will recall his discussion in Part I concerning how evaluative words are more or less meaningless because they are based on individual perspective. For that reason, he argued, 'good' and 'evil' cannot be the basis of any reasonable argument about government – they are simply relative to individual perspective, and therefore changeable and not reliable. It shouldn't surprise us, then, that he views words like monarchy and tyranny in the same way. Hobbes thinks that when a person calls rule by one man a 'tyranny' it simply means that he does not like the monarch. We know that people dislike others often for very personal reasons, having nothing to do with the common good. Hobbes is arguing that we should disregard these pejorative terms as irrelevant at best and dangerous at worst, because such names allow people to criticize their leaders. When this happens, disobedience follows.

Having eliminated from consideration all but monarchy, aristocracy, and democracy, and eliminating any evaluative function of these terms by getting rid of their opposites, he then turns to thinking about which of these three forms is truly the best. It should not surprise us that his analysis consists of the question, how many rulers are best? In other words, he looks at the number of rulers in each case and asks what are the advantages and disadvantages of having that number in charge. He bases his predictions on the assumptions about human nature and behaviour he established in Part I: that people are egoistic, selfish individuals and not social creatures. He does not assume that rulers will be somehow better human beings than those they rule – all human beings can be counted on to be selfish. Hobbes argues that monarchy is superior in all respects to the other two types of government because only in monarchy does selfishness consistently lead the ruler to take care of his people (Mitchell 1993).

For instance, Hobbes argues that the monarchy's private interest in wealth and power coincides with the public's interests. 'The riches, power, and honour of a monarch arise only from the riches, strength and reputation of his subjects' (144). But in an aristocracy or democracy, where rulers have to compete with each other, it is quite likely that the fastest route to power lies in divisive behaviour, like starting rumours about rivals, or even an unnecessary war or civil conflict. Hobbes also argues that advice can be given to a monarch in secret, making it likely that the advice will be honest and also secure. But in an assembly of men, the advice they get will be public, probably in the form of inflammatory rhetoric designed to move the assembly to the particular interests of a part rather than the whole of the commonwealth.

But what if the one man in charge is unstable mentally or emotionally? Hobbes does take this into account, and he seems to conclude that there is some risk, but that the risk of instability in a single person is less than the risk of instability in a group: 'Thirdly, that the resolutions of a monarch, are subject to no other inconstancy, than that of human nature; but in assemblies, besides that of nature, there ariseth an inconstancy from the number. For the absence of a few, that would have the resolution once taken, continue firm, which may happen by security, negligence, or private impediments, or the diligent appearance of a few of the contrary opinion, undoes to-day, all that was concluded yesterday' (144).

First, Hobbes argues, a group can suffer from the instability in human nature, too (as when there is a sort of mob or groupthink mentality), and it also has to contend with instability in its numbers – some members take advantage of the fact that other members are absent when an important decision is being made, or one particular group within the whole is particularly well organized and simply overwhelms the other. Because the monarch is only one person, he is always present, so such intrigues and machinations cannot occur. Hobbes follows up with a similar observation: 'a monarchy cannot disagree with himself, out of envy, or interest; but an assembly may; and that to such a height, as may produce a civil war' (144). Hobbes argues that while monarchs may arbitrarily hurt or help particular individuals, and this is not good, assemblies of men are no better. In fact, there are simply more people who can act in a corrupt and arbitrary manner in assemblies, hurting enemies and helping friends through their political positions and connections.

In Hobbes's sixth argument, he raises a common criticism of hereditary monarchy: that sometimes the next in line for the throne is either an infant or someone otherwise mentally incapable of ruling. In this case, the common practice was to appoint a regent or caretaker over the monarch, who would make decisions until he or she was able to rule effectively. If this person was chosen wisely ahead of time, the risks involved in government by such a monarch were fewer, in Hobbes's view, than the risks involved in government by an assembly of men or by all. In the two other forms of government, the rulers rely constantly on advisors and, for reasons already stated, are more likely to make bad decisions, engage in corruption and so on than government by regent. Here and elsewhere, Hobbes always tackles potential complaints against monarchy with the question, 'compared to what?'

After these arguments, Hobbes turns to demolishing any idea of popular control or limitation of the monarch's power. The power of the monarch must be supreme, because if it is shared or controlled somehow by the popular will, the same dangers associated with these other bodies will still be present and the system will be unstable. Likewise, the monarch must have the absolute right to determine his successor, even if his or her decision ignores regular hereditary lines. If the decision about who should rule next came back to the people, there would be an opportunity for factions to form.[6]

The beginning of the next chapter (20) might confuse readers if they do not keep Hobbes's agenda of obtaining absolute obedience from subjects firmly in mind. Hobbes writes: 'A commonwealth by acquisition, is that, where the sovereign power is acquired by force; and it is acquired by force, when men singly, or many together by plurality of voices, for fear of death, or bonds, do authorize all the actions of that man, or assembly, that hath their lives and liberty in his power' (151).

The first part of this paragraph is clear enough – a commonwealth can be acquired, or taken, by force. But the next part of the paragraph seems a bit harder to grasp, because it seems to have to do with consent. Hobbes says that a commonwealth is acquired by force when people authorize the power which does the forcing. But how can people ever consent to be ruled by something that is forcing them to submit? Later liberal thinkers like John Locke or Thomas Paine found this idea absurd; either people consented freely to be ruled or they were forced. But Hobbes does not see this as an 'either/or' situation. Hobbes is saying that even if consent is given in order to survive, people are still giving their legitimate – and freely willed – consent.

Because they are consenting by submitting, they are bound to obey the power which has forced them. So fear, or what we might call coercion, does not make an agreement invalid. The only way in which commonwealth acquired by force differs from commonwealth by institution (made by a social contract) is that in the first instance people agree out of fear of the one to whom they submit, but in the second they agree out of fear of each other. If fear made agreements invalid, Hobbes states, no commonwealth would be legitimate. Hence, the rights of a sovereign who obtained rule by force are exactly the same as those of a sovereign set up by agreement: they are both absolute. All this has to be so, if Hobbes hopes to effect much change in people's attitudes towards government, because most nations could trace their government's origins to some illegitimate use of force – in England's case, for instance, the Norman Conquest.

Then in the same chapter Hobbes turns to discussing dominion, or power over others, 'paternal and despotical'. Paternal dominion is the power of the father over his family, whereas despotical power is what we just discussed above – power obtained through force. Some, such as Aristotle, would argue that the father's dominion over his family, or at least the family itself, is natural, and that family relationships have nothing to do with consent but come from a much deeper source – nature itself. But Hobbes disputes these notions vigorously, and thus confronts Aristotle again. He says that a father's dominion does not come from the mere 'generation' (the making) of children, but rather 'from the child's consent, either express, or by other sufficient arguments declared' (152).

Hobbes reasons that if generation were the source of dominion over children, then mothers would have just as much right to dominion as fathers. We have already seen that according to Hobbes's logic, men and women, indeed all people, are equal due to their ability in the state of nature to pose a serious threat to each other's lives. Here he adds that there is not enough of a difference of strength or of prudence between men and women 'that the right can be determined without war' (152). He even says that, in nature, the dominion over children would naturally fall to the mother, because unless she says who the father is, no one can be certain of that fact. So, the dominion of fathers over their families is 'decided by the civil law', Hobbes says. It is a matter of agreement, not natural superiority.

The interesting thing about this discussion of the family is that the relationships among the family members in nature are seen by Hobbes as deriving from necessity and consent, and nothing natural. The child owes obedience to whoever nourishes and protects him, whether that person is the mother, father, or a stranger. Fathers can dominate mothers and mothers can dominate fathers. Just as people will submit through fear or need to a conqueror and Hobbes considers this legitimate consent – so in nature people can form 'families' through force. Despotic rule and rule by institution and paternal dominion are all the same type of rule for Hobbes, all equally consented to. The only difference between a family and a kingdom is that a family is not large enough to protect itself adequately if attacked.

Chapter 21 is entitled 'Of the Liberty of Subjects', and in it Hobbes tackles the topic of liberty from several angles. First he defines liberty as not being constrained from freedom of movement – i.e. not being imprisoned or fettered in some way. In defining liberty in this way, Hobbes is disputing those who would argue that people do not have liberty unless they are given certain rights. Instead, he repeats that fear and liberty can co-exist; one can obey the laws out of fear of the sovereign's punishment, but still freely choose to obey the laws. He deals with the philosophical question of whether we really have liberty at all. It would seem that God as the author of all things has predetermined everything that exists, or that what exists now is simply the result of a long chain of causes started by God. Hobbes sees no contradiction. 'And therefore God, that seeth, and disposeth all things, seeth also that the liberty of man in doing what he will, is accompanied with the necessity of doing that which God will, and no more, nor less' (160).

Hobbes reasons that men may do many things contrary to God's will, 'yet they can have no passion, nor appetite to any thing, of which appetite God's will is not the cause' (160). Hence God made man as a choice-making being, and yet he set the parameters of human nature and the physical world and so he would indeed know every choice and action that men might make even though they make the choices freely. Just as the sovereign can constrain the subject with laws and fear of punishment, and yet the subject is seen as obeying by choice, similarly God constrains humanity and yet humanity is free also to choose. This can be quite confusing for readers, but it helps to keep in mind Hobbes's overall goal, which is to prevent his readers from thinking that they have some liberty separate from the authority of their sovereign.

The kind of liberty Hobbes says people have is that which is allowed them by covenants. In other words, by making the social contract, men have submitted to the sovereign's control and they are to see every action of the sovereign (even his punishment of them) as their own. They are then left with the liberty the sovereign chooses to give them. Clearly, the type of liberty Hobbes thinks good and useful is private liberty – the liberty to conduct our private lives for our own good. He does not approve of public liberty – the freedom to interfere in the governing of the commonwealth. Hobbes lists the liberties that are left to citizens as 'to buy, and sell, and otherwise contract with one another; to choose their own abode, their own diet, their own trade of life, and institute their children as they themselves think fit; and the like' (161). These are the liberties of people who have escaped from the barbarism of the state of nature and can begin to build civilization. It is this opportunity to grow and become prosperous because of the relative safety provided by the state that is the *raison d'être* of the social contract.

After taking another jab at the ancient philosophers and historians on the subject of liberty, Hobbes turns to the question of disobedience: are there any areas where a subject can rightfully refuse to obey his sovereign? Surprisingly, perhaps, there are a few. All of them derive from that fundamental right which no one can transfer to another: the right of self-preservation. Subjects always retained the right to defend their own lives when immediately endangered and they cannot be made to hurt themselves. They are not bound to testify against themselves. They cannot be obliged to kill themselves and, more interesting still, they cannot be obliged to kill others. Hobbes's account of military service under these circumstances is worth examining closely:

> Nor to warfare, unless they voluntarily undertake it. Upon this ground, a man that is commanded as a soldier to fight against the enemy, though his sovereign have right enough to punish his refusal with death, may nevertheless in many cases refuse, without injustice; as when he substituteth a sufficient soldier in his place: for in this case he deserteth not the service of the commonwealth. And there is allowance to be made for natural timorousness; not only to women, of whom no such dangerous duty is expected, but also to men of feminine courage. When armies fight, there is on one side, or both, a running away; yet when they do it not out of treachery, but fear, they are not esteemed to do it unjustly, but

dishonourably. For the same reason, to avoid battle, is not injustice, but cowardice. But he that enrolleth himself a soldier or taketh imprest money, taketh away the excuse of a timorous nature; and is obliged, not only to go to the battle, but also not to run from it, without his captain's leave. And when the defence of the commonwealth, requireth at once the help of all that are able to bear arms, every one is obliged; because otherwise the institution of the commonwealth, which they have not the purpose, or courage to preserve, was in vain. (165)

If the whole reason the commonwealth is instituted is for individuals' self-preservation, then individuals cannot be obliged to give up their lives in battle. This seems simple enough, but it leaves Hobbes with a real problem: how can the commonwealth survive and fulfil its purpose of protecting citizens' lives if it does not have a loyal and willing army? Hobbes realizes this problem. He does say at the end of this passage that if the survival of the commonwealth itself is at stake, then everyone is obliged to take up arms in its defence. But this is the same as saying that you have a right to defend yourself when you are being attacked. Under these circumstances, you would be foolish indeed not to defend yourself and others who are also fighting on your side – self-preservation demands it. But in all other cases of war, Hobbes is more equivocal.

What if the king thinks that a neighbouring nation is plotting an invasion and he decides to attack first to protect his citizens from imminent threat? Hobbes cannot say that soldiers are obliged to risk their lives, but he does offer some motivation for doing so: honour. Now as we have seen, Hobbes usually treats honour or pride as harmful. People kill each other over disputes caused by pride. But here, Hobbes acknowledges a good application of pride. He says that when men run away in battle, they cannot be called unjust, but their actions can be seen as dishonourable. Likewise, a man who avoids battle is seen as a coward. Surely these are strong motivations for not running away and fighting bravely even in the face of death. Hobbes also mentions the option of hiring a substitute to fight for another, a practice common in his time, and he notes that if a soldier has been paid to fight, then he is obliged to do so. But in this case we might imagine that the consequences for the mercenary soldier of refusing to fight might simply be loss of pay, or at the most, being brought up on charges of breach of contract. Hobbes's bottom line is that people always have the right to preserve their lives even at the expense of their fellow soldiers and their country, and this remains a problem for Hobbes's ability to establish a well-armed commonwealth even with his allowance for the motivation of honour.[7]

At the end of this chapter, Hobbes discusses the conditions under which subjects would no longer need to obey their sovereign. Again, keeping self-preservation in mind, Hobbes's reasoning becomes clear. If, for instance, the subject has been taken as a prisoner of war, and is given his liberty in exchange for his obedience to a new sovereign, he owes that obedience. He owes no loyalty to a sovereign who cannot offer protection. Just as the child in the state of nature owes obedience to whichever parent or other adult protects him, so the subject should obey whoever protects him. Hobbes makes a distinction between being subdued and being given liberty in exchange for obedience, and being enslaved. Here and elsewhere Hobbes says that if a man is being held by chains or other means, he cannot make a covenant to obey. While Hobbes doesn't say it here, the most likely reason is that a man who is fettered could be killed at any second, and he does not have any private liberty to enjoy. So, Hobbes says that he can try to escape by any means necessary – in this way, he would be working to make his life more secure.

One could argue that this is the 'camel's nose' which allows philosophers such as Locke to claim the right to revolution. Perhaps as soon as Hobbes allows people any justification for disobedience, he is preparing the groundwork for the liberal view that people should evaluate and continually choose their governments. This is not, of course, Hobbes's intention, but it may nevertheless be a problem with his argument.

Chapter 22, 'Of Systems Subject, Political, and Private', deals with the status of various groups and organizations in the commonwealth. The commonwealth itself is a system, one that is independent of other authority. All other human systems or associations are subordinate to the sovereign. Hobbes goes through the various ways people organize themselves, including institutions of government such as parliaments and private institutions for business, society, and pleasure. But his real aim is to identify illegitimate or dangerous systems. Human systems become a threat to the sovereign when they have an 'evil design'. Hobbes mentions business monopolies as a possible example, if they use their monopoly to raise prices on the people in their own country (instead of on other countries, which is another matter). Another example would be a political body exceeding the limits the sovereign has set for it. He says that if a political assembly chooses to do something illegal (outside its set bounds), only those who voted for this action should be deemed guilty. This statement could certainly be seen as a veiled threat to those, like the members of parliament who rebelled against Charles I, who try to make themselves supreme to satisfy their personal ambitions. He also mentions the obvious: secret cabals, feuding families who take the law into their own hands, and other political factions.

There are two things in chapter 23 ('Of the Public Ministers of Sovereign Power') that deserve to be highlighted. This chapter is about the various types of public ministers, such as regents, treasurers, generals, and so on. One point Hobbes makes is that these people, acting in their official capacity, must be obeyed as if they were the sovereign himself. But it is possible 1) that they act only in their private capacity (as when a public official attends a private funeral), or 2) that they may act in a way 'inconsistent with his sovereign power'. Hobbes writes that everyone is obliged to obey these officials unless what they order is 'incompatible with the sovereign's right' (180). This is interesting because it suggests, again, that some judgement is possible and even required on the part of the citizens. Conceivably they could legitimately conclude that an official had overstepped his bounds and should not be obeyed. The other curious item in this chapter is Hobbes's classification of religious ministers as subordinate officials, in the same category as treasurers, generals, and judges. He even describes their mission in a way that obscures its spiritual nature and plays up its social/political function:

> They also that have authority to teach, or to enable others to teach the people their duty to the sovereign power, and instruct them in the knowledge of what is just, and unjust, thereby to render them more apt to live in godliness, and in peace amongst themselves, and resist the public enemy, are public ministers: ministers, in that they do it not by their own authority, but by another's; and public, because they do it, or should do it, by no authority but that of the sovereign. The monarch, or the sovereign assembly only hath immediate authority from God, to teach and instruct the people; and no man but the sovereign, receiveth his power *Dei gratiâ* [by the grace of God] simply; that is to say, from the favour of none but God: all other receive theirs from the favour and providence of God, and their sovereigns; as in a monarchy *Dei gratiâ et Regis* [by the

grace of God and King]; or *Dei providentiâ et voluntate regis* [by God's providence and the will of the King].[8] (181)

Notice that Hobbes refers to religious ministers as teachers. They are to teach the subjects their civic duties and the law (since this is what Hobbes means by just and unjust). In this way they can keep people unified in a common purpose, which is a social good. Hobbes makes sure his readers know where religious ministers receive their authority. They receive it not from God, but from their sovereign. In the midst of this statement, Hobbes tells us that the sovereign receives his power by the grace of God. This may seem like an endorsement of the old 'divine right' theory and a repudiation of the social contract, but we will see that Hobbes does not think the two contradict each other. What he wants to get across here is that only the sovereign is beholden to God, while ministers are beholden to the sovereign. In this way, Hobbes chastises the many clerics of his day who involved their congregations in the civil war.[9]

The next chapter, 'Of the Nutrition, and Procreation of a Commonwealth' (24), plays up Hobbes's original image of the commonwealth as an artificial man. By the nutrition of the commonwealth, Hobbes is referring to commerce, and most of this chapter has to do with buying, selling, importing and exporting, regulation of business, and so on. In a rare instance of agreement with an ancient source, Hobbes quotes Cicero: 'Take away the civil law, and no man knows what is his own, and what another man's' (180). Hobbes wholly disagrees with those who think that there is somehow a natural right to property which originates in the state of nature. Without government, no one's property is secure. The state of nature is a state of poverty and insecurity. Hobbes knows that, at least practically speaking, the sovereign power is itself the ultimate source of all property. He mentions William the Conqueror, who distributed the lands of England among those he favoured. The sovereign has the right to distribute property and the right to redistribute it or take it away. While another subject cannot take a man's property without an agreement between the two, the sovereign who is the source of that property can take it whenever he likes. To say that the sovereign is limited in any way from the ability to take people's property (in a practical sense this usually means taxation) is to cripple the sovereign's power, which as we know is unacceptable to Hobbes (Baumgold 1988: 67–9). This is what Hobbes means by 'The public is not to be dieted.' The sovereign cannot be denied the 'nutrition' he wants, even if his appetite seems unreasonable: 'It is true, that a sovereign monarch, or the greater part of a sovereign assembly, may ordain the doing of many things in pursuit of their passions, contrary to their own consciences, which is a breach of trust, and of the law of nature; but this is not enough to authorize any subject, either to make war upon, or so much as to accuse of injustice, or any way to speak evil of their sovereign; because they have authorized all his actions, and in bestowing the sovereign power, made them their own' (187).

Hobbes refers to the law of nature here. You will recall that he defines laws of nature as rules of reason which people know in the state of nature but cannot reasonably follow. Hobbes has already argued that once instituted, the sovereign power cannot be bound by the laws of nature – so it would seem that these laws have the status of suggestions in the commonwealth, certainly not transcendent laws. The passage above is one of a few where Hobbes tries to show that certain actions of a sovereign could be contrary to these natural laws and thus would be unwise. Hobbes may be attempting to give rulers some advice about how far to push their subjects. Yet at the same time, he always insists that no matter how unwise the sovereign's actions, there is no excuse for disobedience because even these actions are to be considered the actions of all the subjects. We might wonder if Hobbes can have it both ways. Is it possible for subjects to know the laws of nature, see that their sovereign is grossly violating them, and yet not use their judgement against him? Locke thought popular judgement of the sovereign was natural (and healthy), and he disagreed with Hobbes that the social contract bound people to absolute obedience under what he called tyranny. Is Hobbes asking for an impossible level of restraint?

Chapter 25, 'Of Counsel', can be seen as an extension of Hobbes's earlier argument for the superiority of monarchy over aristocracy or democracy. Counsel is best if it is given by one advisor at a time to a single man who can evaluate it and think how best to use it. But counsel becomes mere political rhetoric in assemblies of men. This is what Hobbes is getting at when he notes that 'Exhortation and dehortation' are 'counsel vehemently pressed' (192). When speakers come before an assembly they become emotional, and they try to persuade by means of making others too emotional to make good decisions. This, in his view, is a clear defect in regimes other than monarchy. And even monarchs can get into trouble with counsellors if they listen to them as a group, as they might if they listened to their parliament, or even a group of private advisors. Whenever people are in a group, competition emerges. People use ploys to embarrass their interlocutors. Likewise, they stay silent because speaking might make them more vulnerable to the assault of political opponents. When this competitive dynamic takes over, well-reasoned advice is impossible.

'Of Civil Laws' (26) is one of the lengthiest chapters in Part II, and with good reason. This is where Hobbes distinguishes civil law from other types of law, establishes the source of authority for the civil laws, and dismisses other claims to authority. He first distinguishes counsel from command. The previous chapter was about counsel, but counsel should never be mistaken for command (law). He next defines civil law, reminding his readers that in civil society, it is the same thing as right and wrong (and hence there is no higher moral law): 'Civil LAW, *is to every subject, those rules, which the commonwealth hath commanded him, by word, writing, or other sufficient sign of the will, to make use of, for the distinction of right, and wrong; that is to say, of what is contrary, and what is not contrary to the rule*' (198).

Next, Hobbes states that the sovereign is the legislator or law maker, and he denies any other claims to legislative authority. Remember that the sovereign can be a monarch or an assembly, but wherever the sovereign power resides, there is the law-making authority. So in a monarchy, even though the parliament passes laws, they are to be considered law only because of the monarch's authority. The sovereign has the power to enforce the law or declare it void, and whoever can do this is ultimately the source of the law. As the source, the sovereign cannot be subject to that law, Hobbes reasons, because he or it can change the law at any time. But Hobbes does add that there can be no law if it is not known by the subjects. A sovereign who is so arbitrary as not to let his subjects know his law has not in effect issued any law.

Hobbes restates his earlier argument that the civil law and natural law are one and the same. This is because, in the state of nature, the natural law can be known but not consistently acted upon, because it is not enforced. But the natural law actually indicates the necessity of forming the social contract – it commands to seek peace whenever possible. So the social contract comes out of the natural law, and civil law is then put into place to provide peace. Thus the natural law demands that we obey the sovereign power once it has been created, in order to obtain peace. In this way the civil law will reflect the purpose of the natural law, even if the sovereign sometimes violates particular natural laws, such as gratitude or equity.

Hobbes tries to make it clear that other claims to legal authority are illegitimate. For instance, just because a practice or interpretation of the law is old, that does not give it authority; only the sovereign's will to continue to uphold it gives it authority. Neither are moral philosophers or writers any authority concerning the civil law. Likewise, judges are not the source of law. Their job is to interpret it (according to the will of the sovereign) and to apply it to particular cases. As we have seen, in a monarchy, parliament is not an independent source of law either. This would have been the mistake that worried Hobbes the most, since the English parliament had recently claimed the legislative power for itself and started a war. Tellingly, Hobbes argues that there can be no excuse for misunderstanding where the sovereign power lies – all subjects have the responsibility for knowing this and acting accordingly.

Hobbes acknowledges that all laws need interpretation and states that the interpreters need to be appointed by the sovereign so that they accurately represent his intent. This makes the role of judges and other officials very important. When the sovereign's will is not directly known, Hobbes argues that legitimate interpreters can infer that the sovereign's will is that the laws of nature should be used as guidance. Hobbes compares this straightforward use of judgement on the part of magistrates with the sometimes illogical and destructive application of English common law (based on precedents and previous rulings): '*The sentence of a judge does not bind him, or another judge to give like sentence in like cases ever after. The sentence of a judge does not bind him, &c.* But because there is no judge subordinate, nor sovereign, but may err in a judgement of equity; if afterward in another like case he find it more consonant to equity to give a contrary sentence, he is obliged to do it. No man's error becomes his own law; nor obliges him to persist in it' (206).

In other words, there is nothing sacred or binding about legal precedents. Certainly these precedents cannot be seen as limiting the sovereign's will to do things differently now. Here Hobbes does seem to set the law of nature into a position independent of sovereign authority, especially the law of equity, because he is saying that even the sovereign can make a mistake. But if we remember that even the sovereign's mistakes must be obeyed and are for that time anyway legitimate laws, then this problem can be resolved. Clearly, Hobbes wants good government with reasonable laws and judgments. He even gives some examples of how the common laws of England have been applied in unjust ways:

> Put the case now, that a man is accused of a capital crime, and seeing the power and malice of some enemy, and the frequent corruption and partiality of judges, runneth away for fear of the event, and afterwards is taken, and brought to a legal trial, and maketh it sufficiently appear, he was not guilty of the crime, and being thereof acquitted, is nevertheless condemned to lose his goods; this is a manifest condemnation of the innocent. I say therefore, that there is no place in the world, where this can be an interpretation of a law of nature, or be made a law by the sentences of precedent judges, that had done the same. For he that judged it first, judged unjustly; and no injustice can be a pattern of judgment to succeeding judges. (207)

Hobbes understands that poor and arbitrary judgments like this, which he says are supported by English common law, are not conducive to peace. But peace and good order should be presumed to be the intent of the sovereign when judges are doing their work, unless the sovereign makes his intentions more explicit. Hobbes says a little later, 'Now the intention of the legislator [sovereign] is always supposed to be equity; for it were a great contumely for a judge to think otherwise of the sovereign' (209). Hobbes would never argue for disobeying the sovereign's explicit orders, even if they did seem unjust. But what he is getting at here is that judges may set themselves up, through the use of 'precedent' and other arguments, as independent sources of legal authority, and in doing so they may rule in ways contrary to the interests of the sovereign (and thus of the people, who want peace and good order). Hobbes would certainly not be a fan of 'judicial activism'.

After making a brief comparison of the institutions of the ancient Roman emperor Justinian with English laws and institutions, Hobbes distinguishes natural laws from positive laws. While natural laws are unwritten and eternal, positive laws 'have not been from eternity' but have been made laws by the sovereign, and are written down or in some other way made known. Hobbes then says that there are two types of positive law, human and divine. But given what he has just said that positive law is made law by the sovereign power – it may make the reader wonder, since we usually think of divine law as being made by God. Let us turn to how Hobbes deals with divine positive law and see if we can find out what the relationship is between God's stated laws and the sovereign's authority.

First, Hobbes says that divine positive law is given by God not for all eternity and to everybody, but at a particular place and time for a particular group of people. Such would be the laws given to Moses at Mount Sinai, or the many other laws given to the Hebrews as God's chosen people through Moses and subsequent leaders. Next, Hobbes asks, *'how can a man without supernatural revelation be assured of the revelation received by the declarer?* and *how can he be bound to obey them?'* (212).

To the first question, Hobbes answers very forthrightly that there is no way that we can know for sure that a revelation is true. Either we believe by faith that it is true, or not. But Hobbes notes that no one can be forced to believe when there is no physical proof. 'Miracles are marvellous works: but that which is marvellous to one, may not be so to another' (213). This wry statement leads to another which would especially bother those who believed that religion could be an independent source of truth. Hobbes answers the second question, *'how can he be bound to obey them?'* by saying that a man can be bound by his own assent to the laws, provided the laws do not go against the laws of nature which, after all, are the laws of God. At first, this might seem as though Hobbes is allowing people some independent judgement – at least to determine whether the divine laws he has learned are contrary to the laws of nature and therefore not really divine. But keep in mind that the most important thing about the natural law for Hobbes is that it leads to the creation of sovereignty and obedience. That is why later on Hobbes can state 'a subject that has no certain and assured revelation particularly to himself concerning the will of God, is to obey for such, the command of the commonwealth: for if men were at liberty, to take for God's commandments, their own dreams and fancies, or the dreams and fancies of private men; scarce two men would agree upon what is God's commandment; and yet in respect of them, every man would despise the commandments of the commonwealth' (213–14).

Chapter 27 is called 'Of Crimes, Excuses, and Extenuations'. Here Hobbes puts forth many useful distinctions that would be helpful to anyone interested in the law and how it is applied. This is another example of how, although Hobbes argues that the sovereign power should be absolute, when it comes to how the sovereign should rule, Hobbes's expectations are quite high.

First, Hobbes distinguishes sin from crime. All crimes are sins, but not all sins are crimes. Hobbes gives us his opinion, which would not have been approved of by many Christians of his day, that simply thinking about committing a sin is not a sin. To imagine committing adultery with your neighbour's wife is not a violation of the commandment 'Thou shalt not covet'. To think of ways *actually* to commit adultery, to take any steps either in thought or action to this end, is a sin. But it is not necessarily a crime. It becomes a crime if there is a law against adultery. 'A CRIME, is a sin, consisting in the committing, by deed or word, of that which the law forbiddeth, or the omission of what it hath commanded' (216). So, there can be no crime unless there is a civil power to create and enforce laws. Hobbes makes it clear that people, even in the state of nature, can know the laws of nature, and therefore know right and wrong. But he casts doubt upon the idea that a person could sin in the state of nature by violating these laws. As he explains in this chapter, whatever a person thinks will lead to his survival is excusable in the state of nature. Once in civil society, though, violating laws of nature is a sin. This is true even if the natural law is not reflected in the laws of the commonwealth. Such violation is only a crime if there is a law against it.

Hobbes turns to a common-sense discussion of under what circumstances crimes can be excused or extenuated (partially forgiven). Several times here and elsewhere, Hobbes says that if the laws have not been made known to the people, their ignorance of the law can be an excuse. Ignorance of the penalties for breaking a law is no excuse, since a person should be expected to obey the law regardless of the penalty. On the other hand, if there is a law which the sovereign inconsistently enforces (i.e. when he has treated the crime with 'impunity'), this should at least partly excuse people when they violate the law. Hobbes gives the excellent example of the law against duels; such a law might exist, but alongside a social presumption that any man who does not accept a challenge to a duel is no man. If the sovereign does not consistently enforce the law against duelling and indeed makes it clear that refusing is not shameful but admirable, such practices are bound to continue.

Time after time in this chapter Hobbes sends the sovereign this message: make your laws clear and well known, and be consistent in your application of them and the punishment for their violation, without regard for social class or other distinctions. Indeed, such distinctions are chief sources of disobedience. People in the higher classes should be held to greater accountability for their behaviour instead of less, because their example and teaching provides guidance for those who are weaker. So intellectuals like professors who teach that the law of nature demands rebellion, or that justice can be ignored in favour of self-interest, are more responsible for the crimes that ensue than their followers. As Hobbes puts it, they create a 'scandal'; they scandalize those who look up to them (227). Likewise, those who presume that they are exempt from the laws because they are rich or well connected should be punished more severely for their presumption.

Hobbes notes that people often commit crime because of fear. He wants to make it clear that, even in civil society, if a person wounds or kills another in self-defence, he is to be excused. But if a person wounds or kills another because of some imaginary injury, such as an insult, then he should be held responsible. Likewise, if a man is starving and steals some food in order to survive, he is 'totally excused' (223). Hobbes is very consistent about his bottom-line right to self-preservation.

There is a passage in this chapter that is worth highlighting because of its importance as well as its difficulty:

> If that man, or assembly, that hath the sovereign power, disclaim any right essential to the sovereignty, whereby there accrueth to the subject, any liberty inconsistent with the sovereign power, that is to say, with the very being of a commonwealth, if the subject shall refuse to obey the command in anything contrary to the liberty granted, this is nevertheless a sin, and contrary to the duty of the subject: for he ought to take notice of what is inconsistent with the sovereignty, because it was erected by his own consent and for his own defence; and that such liberty as is inconsistent with it, was granted through ignorance of the evil consequence thereof. But if he not only disobey, but also resist a public minister in the execution of it, then it is a crime; because he might have been righted, without any breach of the peace, upon complaint. (224)

In the second half of this paragraph Hobbes states a general rule that can be used to untangle the rest of the statement. He says that subjects need to notice any order that is inconsistent with sovereignty. So the subject, because he should know that the commonwealth was erected by his own consent and for his defence, ought to be able to recognize an order that subverts his own intentions to create peace – that is, takes away fundamentally from the sovereign power that protects him – and he ought not to obey it! We are left to imagine what kind of order this might be that would contradict the sovereign's absolute power and yet come from the sovereign monarch or sovereign assembly. Perhaps it would be something like telling the subjects to obey the pope in spiritual matters but the sovereign in secular matters. We know that such an act would be contrary to the absolute sovereignty as Hobbes intends it, because it would divide authority and might precipitate civil conflict. Hobbes seems to be advocating disobedience and putting the subject into the seat of judgment about whether a particular law or order preserves the intent of the social contract.

Yet again, Hobbes seeks to soften the implications of this line of reasoning by saying that subjects should not disobey the direct orders of a subordinate officer who is actually trying to enforce the command of the sovereign. Let us say that officers of the king try to force people to attend Catholic mass and the subjects physically resist. Such disobedience would be a crime, Hobbes says, because the subject could have lodged a complaint instead. In other words, it is one thing to petition the sovereign and hope that he rescinds his order; it is another thing openly to disobey, though quiet disobedience in such a situation seems acceptable.

This seems like a muddled teaching, and perhaps it is. But it does point up one aspect of Hobbes's thought that is very intriguing if not easily reconciled with his demand for strict obedience: Hobbes wants to instil a new way of thinking in the common people. He wants them to see themselves as 'owners' of their government, partly responsible for its smooth operation, aware of the principles underlying it, ready to defend it on account of those principles. What he wants is subjects aware enough of their true interests that they actually resist the attempts of elites to subvert the absolute sovereignty of their monarch, even to the point of attempting to discern if their monarch's orders truly reflect the intention of the social contract. But Hobbes seems to be doing something risky here – advocating the political education of the populace and asking them to make such judgements. He seems to think more of their potential for common sense than he thinks of the intellectual machinations of the elite. But when Hobbes moves to this type of argument, he comes perilously close to Locke, who wants the people to judge their government as well and reject it if necessary. The last thing Hobbes wants is rebellion and yet, unintentionally, it sometimes seems as if the seeds of rebellion lie within Hobbes's argument, in cracks such as this.

Chapter 28 is on the subject of punishments and rewards. This chapter is very useful for establishing many common-sense notions of what is appropriate and what is not when it comes to enforcing the law. But the most important part of this chapter is at the very beginning, where Hobbes defines what punishment is. Then he asks how the sovereign got the right to punish his subjects when they are the authors of the contract that brought the sovereign into existence. Hobbes defines punishment as 'an evil inflicted by public authority, on him that hath done, or omitted that which is judged by the same authority to be a transgression of the law. . .' (229). This makes sense, but Hobbes realizes that his readers will quickly begin to wonder how, based on his previous premises, the right to punish subjects could come into the picture. After all, people enter into the social contract to protect their lives. Would they really agree to give their government the power to punish them? Actually, Hobbes believes that they would not. Here is what he says:

> It is manifest therefore that the right which the commonwealth, that is, he, or they that represent it, hath to punish, is not grounded on any concession, or gift of the subjects. But I have showed formerly, that before the institution of the commonwealth, every man had a right to every thing, and to do whatsoever he thought necessary to his own preservation; subduing, hurting, or killing any man in order thereunto. And this is the foundation of that right of punishing, which is exercised in every commonwealth. For the subjects did not give the sovereign that right; but only in laying down theirs, strengthened him to use his own, as he should think fit, for the preservation of them all: so that it was not given, but left to him, and to him only; and (excepting the limits set him by natural law) as entire, as in the condition of mere nature, and of war of every one against his neighbour. (229)

Remember that people make the social contract with each other, not with the sovereign. They promise to give up their right to self-defence in most cases and together they hand over that right to the government they create. But because they contract with each other and do not make an agreement directly with the sovereign, the sovereign is not bound by their intentions. They create a government that is not obliged to them in any way. If it does not protect their lives, as we have seen, they can leave it for another that can. But because there is no contract with the government, the government can do whatever it thinks best. They laid down their arms, and the right to enforce the law, through punishment, is therefore left to the sovereign.

This teaching would seem to sanction just about any act on the part of the sovereign, from the most lenient to the most cruel. But Hobbes does tell us that no one ever actually loses his right to self-defence. If the government comes to punish you, you are at liberty to resist. Hobbes further softens his teaching on punishment by what follows in this chapter. Again, while the sovereign may have the right to do whatever he wishes, that does not mean he should do so. Much of Hobbes's advice in this chapter constitutes good rules for the sovereign to follow. He repeatedly distinguishes between 'hostile acts' towards subjects and legitimate punishments. For instance, to punish someone without charging them and allowing them a trial is an act of hostility, he says, and not a punishment. Likewise, to punish someone for breaking a law that did not exist when he committed the 'crime' is an act of hostility.

In making these kinds of statements, Hobbes seems to back off a little from the vision of the unrestrained sovereign. His distinctions suggest that there *is* a right way and a wrong way to rule. While Hobbes would say that a sovereign should be obeyed even if he is arbitrary, Hobbes clearly does not approve or expect sovereigns in England to act this way. He teaches that arbitrary acts, such as punishing the innocent, result in 'no good to the commonwealth' (234). He argues that such actions violate the laws of nature, giving further proof that Hobbes's laws of nature are strong suggestions for the prudent sovereign.

The next chapter (29) is about the things that tend to dissolve (destroy) a commonwealth. This chapter is classic Hobbes. Here he goes through every trouble-making idea and group that can weaken government and ruin its purpose. Here is a list of these causes of destruction, along with an explanation:

1. '*Want of absolute power*.' If a monarch has claimed less power than he should, either by sharing it, or simply not exercising it,

this can lead to disorder and rebellion, especially if later the sovereign has to become more strict. So the chief cause of breakdown appears to be a weak monarch.

2. *'Private judgment of good and evil.'* When subjects begin to believe that they can judge the actions of the government as good or evil, rebellion is soon to follow. This problem goes along with the first, because a weak sovereign is more likely to encourage this impudence in others. The idea of individual conscience stemming from the Protestant Reformation was a major source of justification for individual judgment of government.

3. *'Erroneous conscience.'* This is the belief that a person must follow his individual conscience, and that if he does not, it is a sin. This again stems mostly from the Protestant Reformation and assumes that people can formulate their own morals and principles based on their understanding of the Bible and their relationship with God. Individuals come to believe they have a moral duty to act upon their conscience. But Hobbes reminds us that 'the law is the public conscience'.

4. *'Pretence of inspiration.'* Another Protestant notion, that *'faith and sanctity, are not to be attained by study and reason, but by supernatural inspiration, or infusion'*. This error is closely related to the third, of course, and is particularly aggravating to Hobbes because no one can prove they have really been inspired. Clearly, Hobbes sides with careful study of the Bible and the use of clear-headed reason, instead of the emotionalism of inspiration.

5. *'Subjecting the sovereign power to civil laws.'* This is the idea that the sovereign should be limited by a set of laws or a constitution. Hobbes again argues that if the sovereign is the sole source of the laws, he cannot be held subject to his own laws.

6. *'Attributing of absolute propriety to subjects.'* This is the idea that people have a right to their private property, and that the sovereign cannot just take it arbitrarily. It goes along with the idea that in order to tax people, you must get their consent. Hobbes would not approve of the motto of the American revolutionaries, 'No taxation without representation!' This would be a severe and unacceptable limit on the power of the sovereign and a source of control for the people. It would lead to a division of interests, which Hobbes so wants to avoid.

7. '*Dividing of the sovereign power.*' Any dividing of the sovereignty into more than one body tends to break down the power
   of the sovereign, because the bodies will naturally become
   pitted against each other. Hobbes discusses the same problem
   under 'Mixed government', below.
8. '*Imitation of neighbour nations.*' This occurs when people
   within one country try to imitate the forms of different governments nearby. Hobbes gives the example of the ancient
   Greek world, and the conflict between Sparta and Athens.
   Hobbes calls Sparta an aristocracy and Athens a democracy.
   Each city tried to get other cities in Greece to adopt its form of
   government in order to create alliances. Hobbes is trying to
   show that neighbouring nations have an interest in changing
   surrounding governments to reflect their own and their interests should be resisted.
9. '*Imitation of the Greeks and Romans.*' This complaint against
   the ancients is nothing new for Hobbes and he repeats the
   reason again here: the ancient Greek and Roman writers
   encouraged democratic and rebellious thought. 'From the
   reading, I say, of such books, men have undertaken to kill their
   kings, because the Greek and Latin writers, in their books, and
   discourses of policy, make it lawful, and laudable, for any man
   so to do; provided, before he do it, he call him tyrant' (241).
   Recall, for instance, that Plato and Aristotle distinguish
   between a monarch and a tyrant, and this is a distinction
   Hobbes rejects.
10. '*The opinion that there be more sovereigns than one in the com-
    monwealth.*' Here Hobbes takes aim mainly at the Catholic
    church and the idea that the sovereign is subordinate to its spir-
    itual authority. It would equally apply to any other claim that
    the sovereign should somehow be constrained by any spiritual
    or other authority. Hobbes remarks: 'a kingdom divided in
    itself . . . cannot stand.'
11. '*Mixed government.*' This is the idea that government's func-
    tions or power can be divided; for instance, that the executive
    and the legislative powers of the government should be divided
    into two separate 'branches' of government, each sharing part
    of the power. Again, this leads to a division of interests which
    Hobbes thinks can lead to civil conflict. Elsewhere, Hobbes
    calls mixed government 'absurd'.

12. '*Want of money.*' Following up on what Hobbes said before about propriety, the sovereign cannot rule effectively if the people withold taxes because of the notion that they should give their consent first.

13. '*Popular men.*' When a subject becomes so wealthy and influential that he could easily lead people against the government, the sovereignty is in danger. This, Hobbes remarks, happens more often in democracies than in monarchies. But we can imagine it would also happen in monarchies where the monarch is weak, as described in the first complaint.

14. '*Excessive greatness of a town, multitude of corporations.*' If a town or other organization of people becomes too great, so that it has enough resources to outfit its own defence, then it has become powerful enough to threaten the sovereign.

15. '*Dissolution of the commonwealth.*' Hobbes adds at the end of the previous section and right before this one that one of the causes of dissolution is 'the insatiable appetite, or βουλιμια [bulimia] of enlarging dominion . . .,' that is, the desire of a sovereign for more and more territory, which may bring about too many 'wounds' on the body politic. This is interesting because it is one of the few causes of dissolution that can be traced back to the sovereign himself (along with the first, weakness). Here at the very end Hobbes adds the obvious; if the state is destroyed by war, the commonwealth is dissolved.

Chapter 30 is the second to the last chapter in 'Of Commonwealth' and in some ways it is the concluding chapter, because the very last chapter serves to lead us into the third part of the book, 'Of a Christian Commonwealth'. It is entitled, 'Of the Office of the Sovereign Representative', and in many ways it is really about the duties of the sovereign, quite apart from his absolute rights. This chapter builds on the intimations of advice that Hobbes has given previously and provides systematic practical instruction on how to govern effectively for the good of the sovereign and the people. Both goods perfectly coincide, in Hobbes's view. He tells us that the sovereign's purpose is the good of the people. He defines this good as their safety, but he also includes in his definition of safety all the things they need to live well: 'But by safety here, is not meant a bare preservation, but also all other contentments of life, which every man by lawful industry, without danger, or hurt to the commonwealth, shall acquire to himself' (247). The sovereign is to concern himself not just with the bare protection of people's lives but also with their welfare, especially their ability to be industrious and to reap the rewards of hard work.

Tellingly, Hobbes uses the word 'duty' in this chapter to discuss what the sovereign should and should not do. Literally, the sovereign *can* do anything he wants, but Hobbes is saying that he *should not* do certain things and he *should* do other things. He reminds the sovereign that he should not give up any rights essential to his being able to protect the people. So the sovereign has a duty to be strong and not to relinquish his power to other people or institutions. Hobbes then reasons that the sovereign has a duty to educate the people about his rights as a sovereign and why he has them. This education, it turns out, is a foremost duty of the sovereign and absolutely essential in Hobbes's view to a well-ordered commonwealth. Here is Hobbes's reason:

> And the grounds of these rights, have the rather need to be diligently, and truly taught; because they cannot be maintained by any civil law, or terror of legal punishment. For a civil law, that shall forbid rebellion, (and such is all resistance to the essential rights of the sovereignty), is not, as a civil law, any obligation, but by virtue only of the law of nature, that forbiddeth the violation of faith; which natural obligation, if men know not, they cannot know the right of any law the sovereign maketh. And for the punishment, they take it but for an act of hostility; which when they think they have strength enough, they will endeavour by acts of hostility, to avoid. (248)

Now we see just how essential education is to Hobbes's plan. He points out here that the rights of the sovereign to exercise his power are as good as the people's acceptance of them. No law can keep people from questioning his rights and not even fear of punishment will do it. Why is this? We have already seen that Hobbes thinks people can be very irrational when they begin to judge government for themselves and think independently about government; pride and malice enter into it, and they do not think well. Once they have come to the point of open criticism of their government, they have gone past the point where laws or even punishment matters. This is why their attitude in general is more important. They must be taught why it is better to be obedient than to think and act rebelliously.

They must be taught what government is really for, namely for their protection and the fostering of their private industry. This is why Hobbes says that the law against rebellion should not be thought of as a civil law at all, as if a written law could prevent people from rebellion. It is more fundamental than that – it is a law of nature and as such known to anyone of sound reason. Once in society, some men will try to seduce others to follow their rebellious plans and that is why this law of nature must always be repeated and taught to all.

The truly interesting and relatively novel idea here is that, in practice, the people's will is continually involved in maintaining the sovereign. Hobbes is saying that the government should educate people to accept its authority, but also as we shall see, should provide them with genuinely good government. As for education, Hobbes maintains that the basic ideas necessary to obtain the obedience of the people are so simple that even the most 'vulgar' can understand them. The problem is that the people listen to their preachers and other prominent men and their ideas are shaped by them. For many, their only exposure to learning is on Sundays at church. So Hobbes aims his arrows directly at the universities, who educate the ministers and other prominent 'opinion leaders'. He remarks that they are the most likely to be arrogant and think it is acceptable to criticize the sovereign. The sovereign has a duty also to make sure that what is taught at the universities supports his power. (So Hobbes is certainly not an advocate of academic freedom!) Hobbes believes the strength of the commonwealth lies with its people and not with its elites. He reasons: 'Potent men, digest hardly any thing that setteth up a power to bridle their affections; and learned men, any thing that discovereth their errors, and thereby lesseneth their authority: whereas the common people's minds, unless they be tainted with dependence on the potent, or scribbled over with the opinion of their doctors, are like clean paper, fit to receive whatsoever by public authority shall be imprinted in them' (249).

This truly remarkable statement is more reminiscent of Enlightenment political philosophy than the early modern period. Hobbes believes the people can be taught what they need to know. They are not so stupid that they cannot learn the basics of political philosophy, especially their duties as citizens. This is in a way a great elevation of their role. It is not the people who are to be blamed for troubles. One gets the sense that Hobbes rather admires the common people when he compares them to the elites: they are honest and most want to work hard and get ahead. They do not naturally want to cause trouble. It is the 'doctors', those with advanced educations and with great ambitions, who want to stir the pot and use the people for their own purposes.

Much of the rest of this chapter has to do with what the people should be taught. Hobbes weaves his suggested political lessons with the great truths of the Ten Commandments, foreshadowing his later teaching that, rightly understood, the Christian religion supports his political science and vice versa. For instance, the first lesson is that the people 'ought not to be in love with any form of government they see in their neighbour nations. . .' (249). Hobbes equates this love of other forms of government with the breaking of the first commandment, 'Thou shalt not have the Gods of other nations . . .' (250). Some other lessons include teaching people not to listen to rebellious men and not to dispute the sovereign power.

Hobbes suggests that opportunities be regularly set aside for teaching the people their duties to the sovereign and to each other. He strongly suggests that these be on Sundays and in church: 'it is necessary that some such times be determined, wherein they may assemble together, and, after prayers and praises given to God, the sovereign of sovereigns, hear those their duties told them, and the positive laws, such as generally concern them all, read and expounded, and be put in mind of the authority that maketh them laws. To this end had the Jews every seventh day, a Sabbath, in which the law was read and expounded . . .' (251). What better place for this regular instruction than church? Knowing that this might be his idea, it is even more understandable that Hobbes ties his lesson plans for the people to the Ten Commandments. There is no important Christian doctrine, in his view, that will not foster proper respect for sovereign authority. But think about what a change this would have been in the relationship between church and state in Hobbes's time, at least in the minds of the clergy. Hobbes wants the churches to be arms of the state. Clergy should not be allowed to preach whatever they want; rather they should be given their 'curriculum', so to speak. Obviously, this challenging view of the relationship between these two institutions is one Hobbes needs to defend at greater length and this is what he begins to do in the next chapter.

But before we leave Chapter 30, there are a few more items worthy of notice. Hobbes criticizes the tendency of kingdoms to promote rather than discourage the inequality of subjects. All should be seen as equal before the sovereign and his law. Indeed, Hobbes argues that those who are great in society should be held to a higher standard of conduct. In any case, it is clear that they should not be given special favours. To this end, he advocates equality of taxes. What he means is that the great should not be allowed to avoid taxes, not that all should pay the same amount. His proposal is that people should pay a tax on what they consume so that those who are wealthy and buy many things will pay more, but those who are either poor or, significantly, more frugal will get taxed less because they consume less. Frugality and the responsible use of resources to build up the economy are attitudes Hobbes wants to encourage.

Hobbes also proposes public charity or welfare in this chapter.[10] He reasons that there will always be those who, through no fault of their own, cannot support themselves. The sovereign should not, he says, 'expose them to the hazard of such uncertain charity' as private donations. Hobbes is not saying that private charity is to be discouraged, but it is not surprising that he does not want to rely on it, given human nature. On the other hand, those who are able to work physically but are not must be 'forced to work' (255). But interestingly, Hobbes's first solution to this problem of idleness is not to use force, but rather to create an environment where the economy can so flourish that there are no excuses for not working. If this does not take care of all the idle people, the next step Hobbes suggests is to send them into other countries that are still wild and undeveloped, i.e. colonization:

> The multitude of poor, and yet strong people still increasing, they are to be transplanted into countries not sufficiently inhabited: where nevertheless, they are not to exterminate those they find there; but constrain them to inhabit closer together, and not to range a great deal of ground, to snatch what they find; but to court each little plot with art and labour, to give them their sustenance in due season. And when all the world is overcharged with inhabitants, then the last remedy of all is war; which provideth for every man by victory, or death. (255)

Notice that Hobbes does not characterize the native inhabitants as any less worthy or equal than the settlers. He only describes a situation like the state of nature, where each is going to try to get what they can. Settlers are not to 'exterminate' the native peoples they find in these places, but rather make them co-exist and introduce the idea of getting as much yield out of a little plot of land as out of a vast expanse. No doubt Hobbes thought that this type of industry made more sense for all. But once the resources are all in someone's possession and there must be competition then, in Hobbes's view, let the strongest win. At least Hobbes's commentary here is not charged with the usual assumptions of superiority and inferiority of cultures usually applied to native peoples. All are truly equal in Hobbes's view and all equally want to survive and prosper.

The final chapter (31) in the second part of *Leviathan* is 'Of the Kingdom of God by Nature'. Hobbes starts out by reiterating his previous arguments concerning the duty to obey the sovereign power. He says that 'subjects owe to [the] sovereign simple obedience, in all things wherein their obedience is not repugnant to the laws of God . . .' (261). The only thing left for Hobbes to explain is 'what are those laws of God'. This question then necessitates a further one. Because knowledge of laws depends on knowledge of sovereign power, we must say something about the Kingdom of God.[11] God's subjects are those who acknowledge his existence and power – all others 'are to be understood as enemies'. This latter statement probably means enemies of God, since the model that Hobbes is using here is still the social contract. All should submit to God and owe him obedience because they recognize his omnipotence. Those who do not are in a state of war with God. They are his enemies.

Hobbes next observes that God speaks to people in three ways: through natural reason, revelation and prophecy. Hobbes says revelation derives from 'sense supernatural' and because no universal laws are possible concerning it (God speaks to individuals in any way he wants), Hobbes removes it from further consideration. He then derives from the other two ways a '*twofold kingdom of God, natural and prophetic*' (262). He identifies the prophetic kingdom with the pact God made with the ancient Hebrews and so he turns to the natural kingdom of God. He defines the natural kingdom in this way: 'natural, wherein he governeth as many of mankind as acknowledge his providence, by the natural dictates of right reason . . .' (262).

Notice that even though Hobbes seems to give almost too much agency to human beings here to accept or reject God's governance, he bases God's sovereignty not on their acceptance but on his omnipotence. Humans obedience is due to God not because of the benefits he gives them (such as life or food) but because of his 'irresistible power' (262). But one might ask, if his power is irresistible, why does his sovereignty depend upon accepting his governance? Hobbes describes a God who is omnipotent in every sense of the word and who has not in the past been loath to show his power, as he did towards Job. There God made it clear, according to Hobbes, that he could afflict people regardless of whether or not they had sinned. His actions are not restrained by our sense of justice.

At any rate, if we are members of the Kingdom of God and as such are under the sovereignty of this omnipotent being, then we must know how to relate to that being. Much of the rest of the chapter is dedicated to what honour and worship people owe to God. It is in this discussion of honour and worship that a large part of Hobbes's agenda is made clear. He quickly comes to the subject of worship and he makes a distinction that clarifies why he entitled his chapter 'The Kingdom of God *by Nature*.': '*Worship natural and arbitrary*. There be some signs of honour, both in attributes and actions, that be naturally so; as amongst attributes, *good, just, liberal*, and the like; and amongst actions, *prayers, thanks*, and *obedience*. Others are so by institution, or custom of men; and in some times and places are honourable; in others, dishonourable; in others, indifferent: such as are the gestures in salutation, prayer, and thanksgiving, in different times and places, differently used. The former is *natural*; the latter *arbitrary* worship' (265).

It is interesting to note that not much later John Locke made a similar argument, but *in favour of* religious toleration. Certain general signs of honour to God are natural, he wrote, but the specific actions of worship that flow from these general signs, such as kneeling or standing, using this or that prayer, were 'indifferent'. That is, they were arbitrarily chosen, man-made, and not natural. Locke thought that because of this, people should not get too concerned about differences in worship styles, prayers, and other forms of worship, but should allow at least various Christian sects the right to worship freely. Hobbes uses the same distinction here, but he uses it in favour of accepting whatever means of worship the sovereign authority orders. If the way we worship is 'indifferent', then we should not worry about submitting to the particular style ordered by the government – we should obey and not fight over such trifles. Hobbes does later put a few qualifiers on this statement. There are some actions that apparently no sovereign could make into signs of respect and worship:

Not all actions. But because not all actions are signs by constitution, but some are naturally signs of honour, others of contumely; these latter, which are the most that men are ashamed to do in the sight of them they reverence, cannot be made by human power a part of Divine worship; nor the former, such as are decent, modest, humble behaviour, ever be separated from it. But whereas there be an infinite number of actions and gestures of an indifferent nature; such of them as the commonwealth shall ordain to be publicly and universally in use, as signs of honour, and part of God's worship, are to be taken and used for such by the subjects. (269)

Hobbes goes through a list of those attitudes which show natural honour and worship and those which do not. And now he is saying that there really are some actions in worship which could not be said to reflect those attitudes and cannot be made a part of Divine worship by any human power (269). Perhaps Hobbes's qualifiers here are just common sense. Who would ever think of making an obvious sign of disrespect into an act of public worship? Only a madman; and yet Hobbes seems to erect a limited standard here which might be taken to restrain what the government could reasonably order.

Near the end of this chapter Hobbes reminds the sovereign and subjects alike of God's 'natural punishments'. This discussion, like that above, seems to fall squarely into the category of sound advice for the sovereign who, after all, is under no other set of laws but the laws of nature. The laws of God are not only apparent to natural reason, but God's natural punishments are also apparent. These natural punishments are common-sense consequences that flow directly from various unwise actions: 'And hereby it comes to pass, that intemperance is naturally punished with diseases; rashness, with mischances; injustice, with the violence of enemies; pride, with ruin; cowardice, with oppression; negligent government of princes, with rebellion; and rebellion, with slaughter' (269–270).

At the very end of this chapter, Hobbes compares himself and his mission directly with that of another very famous and influential philosopher, Plato. He says that he and Plato agree that political disorders will not cease until 'sovereigns be philosophers'. This makes Hobbes wonder if his project can ever possibly succeed, since he is asking for much wisdom on the part of monarchs. He is asking them to rule in a new and different way, to take much more care to reach out to and educate the common people and to leave the intellectuals, religious leaders, and nobility with much less autonomy. So in a way,

Hobbes acknowledges his debt to Plato: he too is a rationalist of sorts, a man who believes in the power of human reason and education to change politics for the better. But unlike Plato, he does not believe that such a vision needs to be so tenuous as to rely on the chance emergence of a philosopher-king. Hobbes says he does not despair about his chances after all, because the thing that distinguishes his thought from Plato's is its relative simplicity. In Hobbes's view, the 'science of natural justice' is the only science the sovereign needs to understand, whereas Plato wanted his leaders to be all-round philosophers, even having to understand the 'sciences mathematical' in order to be true leaders.

Hobbes does not, however, here mention a large difference between his theory of politics and Plato's. Plato's aim was to make leaders and those they led more inwardly moral. But Hobbes's aim is to shape the outward behaviour of both in more productive directions, quite regardless of their inner purity and in fact assuming the self-interest of all involved. Instead, Hobbes cuts short his comparison with Plato and ends by saying that because he has found a simpler science that can be taught more effectively, he has some hope that 'this writing of mine may fall into the hands of a sovereign, who will consider it himself, (for it is short, and I think clear,) without the help of any interested, or envious interpreter; and by the exercise of entire sovereignty, in protecting the public teaching of it, convert this truth of speculation, into the utility of practice' (270).

With this statement, Hobbes places himself in the same position as Aristotle did with Dionysius, as Confucius did with the leaders of Lu, or as Machiavelli did with Prince Lorenzo De Medici. Through his book he hopes to become the advisor to a king and actually to advise many kings. He wants to become the best political advisor by establishing a universal political science, thus providing a permanent solution to the human condition of perennial disorder. That is indeed a grand task!

## Questions

1. Explain how Hobbes disagrees with Aristotle's claim that 'man is a social (or political) animal' by nature. How does he disagree with Aristotle on the types of regimes people can create? Both these disagreements with Aristotle are important for Hobbes's political thought. Why?

2. How is the social contract established and why does Hobbes call it 'Leviathan'?
3. What is the relationship, in Hobbes's view, between the civil law and the laws of nature? What do you think Hobbes's purpose is in discussing the laws of nature in this section?
4. Is there any way, in Hobbes's scheme, that a subject would be justified in disobeying the sovereign power? If so, explain why.

## PART III: OF A CHRISTIAN COMMONWEALTH

In 'Of a Christian Commonwealth', Hobbes explains how the Christian religion relates to the political order and he gives his own unique interpretation of the scriptures.[12] This interpretation is much more closely aligned with Protestant teachings than with Catholicism, but it is nonetheless unique. Hobbes tries to show that there is nothing in the scriptures, rightly understood, that interferes with his political science. In fact, he tries to show that his teachings on government are precisely in accord with and endorsed by properly understood biblical teachings. His efforts were not well received by his contemporaries, whether they were Anglicans, Dissenters, or Catholics. Hobbes often comes across as a sceptic despite his valiant efforts to show that his teachings are in accord with the Bible, but it is an open question whether Hobbes was a true Christian or whether his biblical interpretation is a sincere attempt to ascertain the truth about God. Some scholars have assumed that Hobbes's teachings on the scriptures are merely rhetorical and his serious argument for political order appears in its entirety in Parts I and II of *Leviathan*. Others argue that Hobbes's interpretation of scripture is an integral part of his overall argument and that the first two parts of *Leviathan* could not stand without the last two ('Of a Christian Commonwealth' and 'Of the Kingdom of Darkness') (Cooke 1996: 203–5).[13] One thing is clear: Hobbes wishes to cut the ground of independence out from under those who would shake the foundations of sovereignty: Catholics on the one hand and dissenting Protestants on the other. Stephen State summed up his intent in this way: 'Whereas Catholics might wish to follow the Pope and some Puritans might wish to follow private opinion or men chosen by apparent grace on matters of religion, Hobbes defends sovereign authority on religious matters by means of his philosophically informed Scriptural exegesis' (State 1987: 91).

The first chapter, 'Of the Principles of Christian Politics' (32), begins by noting that previously Hobbes has tried to establish his political science on the basis of natural reason alone, but now he is going to turn to the Christian commonwealth, whose nature and rights depend 'much upon supernatural revelations of the will of God . . .'. So, 'the ground of my discourse must be, not only the natural word of God, but also the prophetical' (271). Notice that Hobbes still includes natural reason as good for reasoning about the Christian commonwealth: he is not turning to prophecy alone, but to a combination of reason and prophecy. Using natural reason, for instance, he tells us how we should think about scriptural passages that do not seem to make sense. If they do not make sense, it is only because we have not used enough skill in interpretation or we have not been reasoning well enough about them.

Next Hobbes offers a wry observation on the nature of the relationship between reason and biblical revelation and prophecy:

> Therefore, when any thing therein written is too hard for our examination, we are bidden to captivate our understanding to the words; and not to labour in sifting out a philosophical truth by logic, of such mysteries as are not comprehensible, nor fall under any rule of natural science. For it is with the mysteries of our religion, as with wholesome pills for the sick; which swallowed whole, have the virtue of cure; but chewed, are for the most part cast up again without effect. (271–2)

Hobbes is saying that when it comes to religious mysteries, sometimes the more you think about them or 'chew' on them, the harder it is to accept them. But if you believe them uncritically, they can still do you some spiritual good. This is certainly an ironic statement coming from Hobbes. He is about to chew his way through various religious beliefs and biblical teachings and reason about them until some of them are eliminated entirely and others are changed almost beyond recognition for the traditional believer. Hobbes is not one to swallow anything whole, nor does he believe others should do so. And here he rather honestly points out that such chewing can lead to disbelief! On the other hand, he may end up concluding that swallowing religious teachings whole might be more conducive to the sovereignty of the Christian commonwealth and to Christian faith.

In this same chapter, Hobbes casts doubt upon the validity of prophecy itself, by questioning how a man can know that another man has spoken with God, or had a prophetic dream or vision. The man could have had a simple dream, he reasons, or he could have had a sort of day-dream. If a man says he has had a revelation, it simply means that he has a strong desire to talk about what he thinks, because he thinks so highly of himself! Indeed, Hobbes comes right out and says that such a man may not just be in error, but may indeed be lying about having had a revelation. How, Hobbes asks, can we tell a true prophet from a false one? Drawing from scriptural quotations, he says that a true prophet is one who performs miracles and who does not teach 'any other religion than that which is already established' (273). This latter criterion is no doubt aimed at the many preachers who spoke prophetically in his own day and who spoke against the primacy of the established Church of England. However, when you apply these criteria to the prophets of the Bible's Old Testament, such as Abraham, who brought monotheism into a polytheistic world, or even Jesus Christ in the New Testament who certainly brought about a radically new interpretation of Judaism, it becomes hard to know if there have ever been any true prophets. Clearly, Hobbes is warning people away from would-be prophets who criticize the king – he reminds his readers of the many warnings Christ himself raised about the future coming of false prophets and false Christs. As State says, 'When Hobbes undertakes to circumscribe prophetic discourse and undermine belief in the contemporary possibility of miracles he is not inventing a secular world. Like [Anglican theologian] Hooker he is protecting a state church from the volatile incursions of inspiration and zeal' (1987: 88). But despite his religious or political intentions, the overall effect of Hobbes's teaching on the sources of faith in religion is to promote a religious scepticism that has broader implications.

Hobbes points out that miracles long ago stopped happening and so there can be no modern prophets anyway, according to his criteria. He concludes: '*Miracles ceasing, prophets cease, and the Scripture supplies their place*' (275). He turns to scripture for his information and will subject it to rigorous interpretation and reasoning. Hobbes claims that a person does not need any supernatural inspiration or 'enthusiasm' to understand his duty either to God or man; he only needs to read the scripture.

Chapter 33 displays Hobbes's knowledge and thinking about the scripture. Significantly, he starts out by claiming that it is the sovereign's role to identify canonical books of the Bible. 'Canonical' means to be deemed true and authoritative. Thus it is only logical that Hobbes can only acknowledge those books accepted as canonical by the Church of England. It is to these books Hobbes turns next. One point Hobbes makes repeatedly is that the scriptures are not authored by those often named in their titles. The books attributed to Moses were not written by Moses, but by someone who came later, but who had knowledge of what Moses did and said. The book of Joshua was not written by Joshua, but by someone 'long after the time of Joshua . . .' (278). Hobbes finds evidence for this in the texts themselves. For instance, in the book of Joshua, the author says 'The place is called Gilgal unto this day', which certainly implies that the book was written long after the events it chronicles (278). He concludes that the entire Old Testament was written down after the Babylonian captivity.[14] This idea would have been new and very challenging to many of the believers of Hobbes's day and might have had the effect of casting the veracity of the books into doubt.

Hobbes then turns to the New Testament, which deals with Christ's life and teachings. Here it is important to look at a key passage. After stating that the writers of the New Testament all lived in the same general time period as Christ and had except for two seen Jesus with their own eyes, Hobbes turns to the role of the Catholic Church in compiling the New Testament scriptures:

> The Council of Laodicea is the first we know, that recommended the Bible to the then Christian churches, for the writings of the prophets and apostles: and this Council was held in the 364th year after Christ. At which time, though ambition had so far prevailed on the great doctors of the church, as no more to esteem emperors, though Christian, for shepherds of the people, but for sheep; and emperors not Christian, for wolves; and endeavoured to pass their doctrine, not for counsel and information, as preachers; but for laws, as absolute governors; and thought such frauds as tended to make the people the more obedient to Christian doctrine, to be pious; yet I am persuaded they did not therefore falsify the Scriptures, though the copies of the books of the New Testament, were in the hands of the ecclesiastics; because if they had had an intention to do so, they would surely have made them more favourable to their power over Christian princes, and civil sovereignty, than they are. (282)

Hobbes concludes that he sees no reason to doubt the truth of the New Testament scriptures, but nevertheless he has given ammunition for doubt. Part of his purpose is to demonstrate the place in time when early Christianity began to veer from the truth; that is, when the Catholic church began to assert any independence from and control over Christian princes, when it began to show its own political ambitions. He characterizes the Catholic church as being driven by the desire for power. He even accuses the authorities of the Church of committing 'frauds' in order to make the people more obedient. But in the end he makes a statement which is more about his own reading of the scriptures. His reading supports his political philosophy and does not at all support the idea of an independent or authoritative church. At the same time, however, the reader cannot help but feel a little confused about the New Testament scriptures. If they were compiled by an ambitious church capable of perpetrating fraud in order to keep their people in line, then how can we be so sure that the New Testament is really authentic? In this and in his earlier discussion of the authorship of the Old Testament, the upshot of Hobbes's discussion is to cast doubt and confusion on the scriptures. If this is so, it certainly complements the message with which he began his chapter: that we must take as canonical only what our sovereign tells us is canonical. As we will see, obeying the sovereign is a safer course by far than following the will of God by attempting to interpret scripture.

Next, in chapter 34, Hobbes takes on the 'schools' (universities), and in particular their loose use of terminology. Here Hobbes shows his rather strict materialism. Since Hobbes does not believe that anything can exist that does not take up physical space, he rejects the intellectuals' use of terms such as 'immaterial substances' or 'incorporeal' entities as so much nonsense. These terms are actually, in his view, *contradictions* in terms. But of course these are the words the university professors, still influenced by older Catholic scholarship, used to describe the indescribable – their conceptions of the spiritual world.

Hobbes explores several possible causes of what people call 'spirits'. They may be dreams, or they may be products of a disturbed ('distempered') mind, or of a disorder or confusion in our bodily senses. Or they may have physical causes which we cannot explain. People call these things spirits or ghosts, but they are nothing, or at least nothing of the sort. The word 'spirit' can be used in the metaphorical sense, though. If it is used in this way, it is not inaccurate or nonsensical. It means a frame of mind or disposition, such as the 'spirit of wisdom'. Hobbes examines the way that 'the Spirit of the Lord' or 'the spirit of God' are used in the Bible. In biblical passages where the 'Spirit of God' means God Himself, Hobbes says, 'the place falleth not under human understanding; and our faith consisteth not in our opinion, but in our submission. . .' (287). Hobbes finds many places where even these types of phrases can be interpreted as a frame of mind, or of some physical event such as the blowing of the wind. But still, there are some places in the Bible where it seems difficult to attribute to them either of these meanings to them, as when the Bible mentions angels. In this case, Hobbes combines his acceptance of the truth of the biblical canon with his strict materialism and proclaims that these must be spirits that have bodily substance as well:

> And some such apparitions may be real, and substantial; that is to say, subtle bodies, which God can form by the same power, by which he formed all things, and make use of, as of ministers, and messengers, that is to say, angels, to declare his will, and execute the same when he pleaseth, in extraordinary and supernatural manner. But when he hath so formed them, they are substances, endued with dimensions, and take up room, and can be moved from place to place, which is peculiar to bodies; and therefore are not ghosts *incorporeal*, that is to say, ghosts that are in *no place*; that is to say, that are *nowhere*; that is to say, that seeming to be *somewhat*, are *nothing*. (291)

This insistence on the physicality of all things runs throughout Hobbes's work and takes on special significance in this part of the book. Notice that Hobbes affirms God's omnipotence: God can make anything he wants to, for any purpose. He does not have to do this through natural means; he can use 'supernatural' means, that is, means other than the natural processes we see at work in the world. So Hobbes is affirming that God can do anything he wants to, even miraculous things. Yes, God can send dreams and visions to carry a message and he may also send angels. All Hobbes is saying is that when God creates angels or anything else, they must be substantial, tangible, real. Hobbes believes that much of the language of professors of religion and philosophy, and much of the talk of clerics, is vague and mysterious. The motive for this ambiguous language is to keep the common man in awe of their ability to fathom the unfathomable. This is definitely a power he wants to take away from these over-rated authorities. He wants to make their language look silly, which is probably the reason for all the 'that is's' at the end of this passage!

The next word whose definition Hobbes challenges and attempts to clarify is 'inspiration'. Literally this word means 'blowing in', he says, as in the blowing in or putting in of a spirit. But Hobbes claims that this word should always be understood in the metaphorical sense. He denies in a number of ways that it means God's pouring or blowing in of some actual spiritual substance in people. Rather it means God's actions in the world. For instance, the Bible says that God '*inspired* into man the breath of life', but this just means that God gave man life and does not indicate that he did this by blowing in some substance. In this way, Hobbes takes a further turn in his materialistic understanding of the Bible. In his treatment of inspiration he excludes one of the two categories of meaning he discussed when writing about spirits. Here only the metaphorical meaning is left, and the possibility of something physical ruled out, even though God can do anything he wants.

Central to his unique interpretation of the Bible and formulation of his own theology is the next chapter, 35, which deals with 'The Signification in Scripture of the Kingdom of God, of Holy, Sacred, and Sacrament'.[15] Hobbes notes that most clergy and professors of religion take the scriptures' references to the 'kingdom of God' metaphorically to mean Heaven, or sometimes for a sanctification in this world, but 'never for the monarchy, that is to say, the sovereign power of God over any subjects acquired by their own consent, which is the proper signification of kingdom' (297). First, Hobbes claims that references to the 'kingdom of God' in the scriptures do refer to a real kingdom, that is, the monarchy he described above. Second, the monarchy that the Bible refers to is the one established in Israel, the result of a covenant between God and Abraham and then renewed in God's covenant with Moses.[16]

If you are not familiar with these Bible stories, what is important here is that Hobbes is looking to the original establishment of monotheism as the establishment of the 'kingdom of God.' Abraham is the figure credited in the book of Genesis with being first chosen by God and then making a covenant with God. The agreement was that the new people, Abraham's family and their descendents, would obey God's laws and serve only the one true God. In exchange, God would bless them. To Moses, God promised the Holy Land in exchange for the continued obedience of the Jewish people. At a certain point in Jewish history, the Hebrews asked God for an earthly king, so that they could be more like their neighbours. God obliged, making Saul their king and withdrawing (in Hobbes's view) from his role as king. At this point, Hobbes claims, the 'kingdom of God' came to an end.

Hobbes turns to the role of Jesus in the New Testament, and there he sees evidence for his interpretation. There, 'the angel Gabriel saith of our Saviour (*Luke* i. 32, 33) *He shall be great, and be called the Son of the most High, and the Lord shall give unto him the throne of his father David; and he shall reign over the house of Jacob for ever; and of his kingdom there shall be no end*' (300). Hobbes notes that Jews at the time of Jesus' death thought that he was the one who would come back and reinstitute God's real kingdom on earth and he surmises that Jesus was crucified precisely because he was a threat to Roman power. Hobbes turns to the prayer Jesus taught his disciples, commonly known as the Lord's Prayer, which pleads in part 'Thy kingdom come'. Hobbes reasons, if God always had a kingdom, why would Jesus have instructed his followers to pray for God's kingdom to come? Hobbes sums up his reasoning in this way:

> In short, the kingdom of God is a civil kingdom; which consisted, first, in the obligation of the people of Israel to those laws, which Moses should bring unto them from Mount Sinai; and which afterwards the high-priest for the time being, should deliver to them from before the cherubims in the *sanctum sanctorum* [the holiest part of the temple]; and which kingdom having been cast off in the election of Saul, the prophets foretold, would be restored by Christ; and the restoration whereof we daily pray for, when we say in the Lord's Prayer, '*Thy kingdom come*'; and the right whereof we acknowledge, when we add, *For thine is the kingdom, the power, and glory, for ever and ever, Amen* . . . (301)

In Hobbes's view, then, the kingdom of God will only come again when Christ returns to earth. In the meantime there is no kingdom of God in the sense that God rules humankind directly. As we know already, Christians are supposed to take their cue from the sovereign power about what to believe, how to worship, what biblical books are canonical and how to interpret them. Hobbes's teaching about how to understand the references to God's kingdom goes along well with this view of sovereignty in spiritual matters. When

Saul became king, God in effect handed over the reins of power to earthly leaders. Therefore there is no conflict between obedience to earthly authorities and the priorities of the 'kingdom of God', since that kingdom does not currently make any direct demand for obedience.

As Mitchell explains, Hobbes thought that when the people of Israel chose a king, they broke the covenant with God and made a new one:

> The kings retained their right to judge in matters both sacred and profane, like Moses and the prophets before them; but because the people no longer understood the reason for it, the covenant disintegrated. . . . Christ then prepares the way for a renewal of the covenant with God, for the instauration of sovereign authority where the people obey their sovereign in all matters and know the reason for it. Christ, in a word, prepares the way for human beings not to contest with their sovereign as the Israelites did when they no longer knew why they owed him obedience. (Mitchell 1991: 690–1)

According to Mitchell, Hobbes's thought differed from Luther's here. Luther believed that the New Testament superseded the Old Testament. But for Hobbes, the New Testament renewed the covenant made to Abraham and Moses in the Old Testament. Because Hobbes saw the Catholic church as a flawed vessel for God's purpose (he identified it with the 'kingdom of darkness', as we will see), Christ's renewal of the covenant did not occur with the conversion of the Roman emperor Constantine, but only came to fruition in Hobbes's day and Hobbes's England. *So Hobbes's England is the true Christian commonwealth*: 'It is finally in England, then, that the kingdom of darkness comes to an end. Not at the time of Constantine, but at the *present* moment is Christ's covenant properly renewed. Here is nothing less than a vision of England's significance in the unfolding of biblical history. God's trace, once lost, is reinstated' (Mitchell 1991: 692).

If Mitchell's view of this is correct, than Hobbes's theological teachings on the renewed covenant really are nothing short of indispensable to his political theory.

In 'Of the Word of God, and of Prophets' (chapter 36) Hobbes argues against the literal interpretation of the Bible's references to Jesus as the word of God, and discusses how one can tell between true and false prophets. The first argument appears fairly uncontroversial, and shows us again Hobbes's wry sense of humour. At one point Hobbes says that a too-literal understanding of the 'word of God' is just as silly as calling Christ the 'noun of God' (306). On the serious side, Hobbes is arguing against literalism in his treatment of the Bible, because many things in the Bible, if taken literally, would strain his ability to believe. But the more controversial part of this chapter is Hobbes's treatment of prophets and prophecy.

Hobbes knows that people who claim to have a direct knowledge of God's will, or claim to have spoken with God, can move believers in God to do many things. Prophecy is a powerful tool in the hands of good as well as bad leaders. He defines a prophet as someone who speaks for God. But he warns that not everyone who claims to be a prophet is one. Indeed he warns that the sign most taken for prophecy, the prediction of future events, can just as easily be done by 'impostors, that pretend, by the help of familiar spirits' (308) (demons, for instance) to know the future. He points out that the Bible makes frequent references to false prophets and prophecy and warns people against them.

How does God really speak to men? This is what Hobbes asks first. He discusses the various ways featured in the Bible and he finds no evidence that God speaks directly, as human beings would do, with his own voice and in his own presence. Indeed, even Moses, the most special prophet of God who brought the Jews the Ten Commandments, did not in Hobbes's view have that direct experience. Hobbes refers to the burning bush from which God spoke to Moses on Mount Sinai as an 'apparition of a flame of fire out of the midst of a bush' (310). God also spoke to Moses through angels. But in any case, even Moses' encounters with God were 'a vision, though a more clear vision than was given to other prophets' (311). We know that for Hobbes visions are a type of dream. We know also that Hobbes thinks that visions or dreams can be products of God's will – or products of indigestion – and that it is impossible for the outside observer to tell whether the source is supernatural or natural. So even though Hobbes categorizes Moses as a 'supreme' prophet and therefore on a high level of credibility, even with Moses the divine origins of his prophecy cannot be validated without faith. Eventually Hobbes concludes that it is 'not intelligible' how God communicated with Moses and so he leaves the acceptance of Moses' authority in the realm of faith.

In contrast with the supreme prophecy of Moses, there are the sub-ordinate prophets. Hobbes found no evidence that God spoke to them in any supernatural way. These men are to be considered prophets only in the sense that their knowledge of God allowed them to speak in an instructive manner about him. Thus Hobbes makes it possible for us to see a prophet as someone who is knowledgeable about God and Christ's teachings and does not need to have any supernatural experiences like visions in order to teach people about God. This leads Hobbes to pay more attention to the message rather than the messenger when it comes to prophecy. Hobbes reasons that good Christians must be able to discern true prophecies from false. Since they cannot know with certainty whether or not a man has received a supernatural communication, and since prophecy does not have to entail such communication anyway, the measure of a prophet's truthfulness must be in his message. The message must be conformable to biblical truth (as Hobbes defines it). Hobbes wants his readers to be very wary when it comes to prophecy. In this way, Hobbes seems to be encouraging some independence of thought among the common people in an effort to dissuade them from being led by the charlatans of his own day.

> Every man ought to examine the probability of a pretended prophet's calling . . . there is need of reason and judgment to discern between natural, and supernatural gifts, and between natural, and supernatural visions or dreams. And consequently men had need to be very circum-spect and wary, in obeying the voice of man, that pretending himself to be a prophet, requires us to obey God in that way, which he in God's name telleth us to be the way to happiness. For he that pretends to teach men the way of so great felicity, pretends to govern them; that is to say, to rule and reign over them; which is a thing, that all men naturally desire, and is therefore worthy to be suspected of ambition and impos-ture; and consequently, ought to be examined and tried by every man, before he yield them obedience; unless he have yielded it them already, in the institution of a commonwealth; as when the prophet is the civil sovereign, or by the civil sovereign authorized. (314–15)

Is Hobbes really advocating independent judgement of prophecy and religious teachings? At first it seems so, because Hobbes advises us to be very suspicious of those who claim to speak for God. He provides a way of seeing these prophets that is designed to rid his readers of their innocence, if indeed they still have any. A prophet (preacher) who tells his followers that he has found the way to felicity (happiness) is telling them what to believe and what to do. We already know that all men want power, so anyone who makes such claims should be examined carefully and suspected of 'imposture', or trying to replace legitimate authority. But all is different if the civil sovereign, the true legitimate source of authority, has approved of the teachings of a particular preacher. This latter point mitigates any sense in which Hobbes is calling for independent judgement. In the end, the best way to judge whether or not a prophecy or other religious teaching is true is to ask whether or not the prophet or teacher has official sanction. Ultimately, the judgement of true or false, right or wrong, remains in the sovereign's control, not the individual's. Any other position on the source of truth will lead to disorder, both social and moral:

> For when Christian men, take not their Christian sovereign, for God's prophet; they must either take their own dreams, for the prophecy they mean to be governed by, and the tumour of their own hearts for the Spirit of God; or they must suffer themselves to be led by some strange prince; or by some of their fellow-subjects, that can bewitch them, by slander of the government, into rebellion, without other miracle to confirm their calling, than sometimes an extraordinary success and impunity; and by this means destroying all laws, both divine and human, reduce all order, government, and society, to the first chaos of violence and civil war. (317)

In subsequent chapters, Hobbes will reason that this over-lordship of the truth is God's will and that the Bible rightly understood supports the full and exclusive authority of the sovereign on all such matters. Part of this argument will derive from the theology he has already developed, which states that the 'kingdom of God' was a covenant that was broken by the Jews at the time of King Saul and that will come again with the second coming of Christ, but in the meantime the social contract that constitutes the sovereign power has the ultimate authority on earth. He will explain that this is all God's will and that God's representative on earth today is not a prophet or preacher but the legitimate head of government.

Hobbes's next chapter is on miracles. You may recall that in the very first chapter of this third part of *Leviathan* on the Christian commonwealth, Hobbes stated that miracles had ceased in modern times. Indeed, he concluded that *Miracles ceasing, prophets cease, and the Scripture supplies their place* (275). But in this chapter (37), Hobbes revisits the issue of miracles and discusses their purpose and how to distinguish a true miracle from one that is false. One may wonder why he needs to do this, but Hobbes knows that many people may still be led to believe in present-day miracles despite his determination that none exist. If this is the case, Hobbes may think it useful to make his readers more sceptical about claims to miraculous healings, signs and other similar modern-day miracles. While they continue to believe in the power of God to do whatever he wants in the modern world, Hobbes's readers may become more dubious about the motives of their fellow man. The sceptical subject, in Hobbes's view, is to be preferred to the gullible subject, especially if the sceptic is armed with Hobbes's full political philosophy.

Hobbes defines a miracle as something having no ordinary natural cause and performed directly by God. He tries to show that there are many things which might appear strange or unnatural to us, but can nevertheless have natural causes if we only examine them carefully (such would be the case with eclipses). What seems miraculous to one man does not seem so to another man and the difference is actually in their relative levels of knowledge of natural causes, that is, in their relative levels of education. The end or purpose of a real miracle, Hobbes reasons, is 'for the procuring of credit to God's messengers, ministers, and prophets, that thereby men may know, they are called, sent, and employed by God, and thereby be the better inclined to obey them' (319). Miracles must be truly supernatural and they must have the purpose of pointing the way to true representatives of God. Hobbes points out that many acts of 'conjuration' or magic may seem like miracles, but are really the products of human ingenuity. They do not serve the proper purpose – to elevate God's representatives – and this should give people a clue that they are false.

Hobbes dwells for quite some time on the miracles performed by Moses in Egypt. These miracles served the purpose of showing God's preference for Moses as his representative and they eventually frightened the Pharaoh into letting the Jews leave Egypt. However, the Bible states that the Pharaoh's magicians were able to replicate many of Moses' miracles with their own magic. This shows that the purpose of the miracle is a more important sign of its truth than its seeming to be supernatural. So even when discussing Moses' miracles, Hobbes wants people to think critically. He cautions his readers 'that we take not any for prophets, that teach any other religion, than that which God's lieutenant, which at that time was Moses, hath established . . .' (323). We already know that since the time of Saul, God's lieutenant has been the earthly sovereign. So here is the question one must ask to decide on the validity of a miracle: does the sovereign say it is to be believed? While Hobbes does not want to name 'God's lieutenant' here in this chapter but wants to wait until he can further justify the sovereign's status as such in another chapter, clearly he is suggesting that 'God's lieutenant' is the ruler of the land – not any mere religious leader.

Hobbes picks an easy target to give an example of appropriate scepticism: 'For example; if a man pretend, after certain words spoken over a piece of bread, that presently God hath made it not bread, but a god, or a man, or both, and nevertheless it looketh still like bread as ever it did; there is no reason for any man to think it really done, nor consequently to fear him, till he enquire of God, by his vicar or lieutenant, whether it be done, or not' (323).

Hobbes uses the anti-Catholicism of the majority of Anglicans and Protestants at this time to make his point about the manipulative nature of some men and the gullibility of others. He is referring here to the Catholic belief in transubstantiation: that in the celebration of the Eucharist, bread and wine become the Body and Blood of Jesus Christ, despite the fact that the outward appearance of the bread and wine are the same. Hobbes will use this tactic repeatedly; he will attack various Catholic beliefs and practices and argue for their lack of credibility because 1) so many of his fellow Englishmen will find it easy to agree with these examples, and 2) through them, Hobbes can further develop an appropriate degree of scepticism to all claims of miraculous and mysterious occurrences. In other words, if Hobbes can associate belief in miracles and mysteries with unpopular Catholicism, then it will be easier for his readers to accept and adopt his sceptical attitude to all such claims, Catholic or Protestant. Of course, the true trouble makers in Hobbes's day were not the Catholics but Dissenting Protestants, whose claims to 'inspirations' from God allowed them more easily to lead the people according to their political agenda.[17]

Hobbes next turns to the grandest of subjects – Heaven and Hell. This is one of the most breathtaking and dangerous parts of *Leviathan*. It is breathtaking in its object and scope; here Hobbes purports to teach his readers the truth about the existence and nature of the afterlife, according to his interpretation of the Bible. It is dangerous because it challenges so many devout beliefs and literally brings Heaven (and Hell) down to earth. Early on in this chapter (38 – 'Of the Signification in Scripture of Eternal Life, Hell, Salvation, the World to Come, and Redemption') Hobbes provides a disclaimer of sorts: '(with submission nevertheless both in this, and in all questions whereof the determination dependeth on the Scriptures, to the interpretation of the Bible authorized by the commonwealth, whose subject I am)'. But he goes on to interpret the Bible on these issues in such a way as to make Heaven less impressive and Hell less terrifying in the minds of his worried readers (or so he hopes). He indicates his agenda quite forthrightly at the beginning. If there is some other authority that can give greater rewards than life or greater punishments than mere death, then the authority of the sovereign is diminished and it is impossible to rule. So if an authority such as the church claims to be able either to guarantee Heaven or send a person to Hell, that authority will be more impressive than the sovereign. After all, who would not be more concerned with everlasting life and death than with the temporary joys and punishments of this world?

Knowing his agenda is to make sure that no other authority threatens the legitimate authority of the sovereign will help the reader understand this chapter. Hobbes argues that the place people will go to live out the rewards of faithfulness for all eternity will be here on earth. He reasons that if Adam had not sinned, he would have remained in Paradise forever, and that Paradise was on earth. So, Hobbes reasons, the restored Paradise will also be on earth, God's 'footstool'. Hobbes provides many Scriptural passages to prove his point that Heaven is not some place beyond but will be here, reinstituted at the second coming of Jesus Christ. At that time, all men will be resurrected and those who are chosen by God will live forever in an earthly Paradise. It will be a kingdom because at that time Christ will rule as an earthly sovereign over his people. It will be a kingdom of Heaven because it will be God's kingdom on earth. This interpretation goes along well with Hobbes's well-established materialism. Hobbes believes that our existence after death remains a physical, earthly existence. The resurrection will truly be of the body – either that, or there would be no logical way to exist at all.

So far, so good. Hobbes's teachings on Heaven, while they might have seemed strange to many, at least seem to confirm that those who remain faithful to God will enjoy everlasting life. But we have yet to look at what Hobbes says about Hell. When it comes to the place that most people held to be involved in everlasting punishment, Hobbes has some rather surprising and perhaps pleasing news. Hobbes again goes through various Bible passages to show that Hell, too, must be a physical, earthly place. All people, when they die, are in the ground awaiting the return of Christ and the resurrection. But when the resurrection happens, those who have not lived faithful lives and are not chosen by God for eternal life must go to Hell. However, Hobbes argues that the Bible's references to what Hell must be like – a lake of everlasting fire, or a place of utter darkness – must be taken metaphorically and the Bible's words need to be understood with more care than most people usually give them. For instance, Hobbes points out that the Bible's reference to 'utter darkness' is more accurately translated as 'external darkness' or 'darkness without', which really means that those in Hell will be in another place separate from those whom God has saved (the elect) (331).

Hobbes next argues that the names 'Satan' and 'Devil' are not proper names of specific beings but rather 'appellatives' which describe the function they serve. If this is the case, then these words mean something far different from what many believers in Hobbes's time thought:

> And because by the Enemy, the Accuser, and Destroyer, is meant the enemy of them that shall be in the kingdom of God; therefore if the kingdom of God after the resurrection, be upon the earth, as in the former chapter I have shown by Scripture it seems to be, the Enemy and his kingdom must be on earth also. For so also was it, in the time before the Jews had deposed God. For God's kingdom was in Palestine; and the nations round about, were the kingdoms of the Enemy; and consequently by Satan, is meant any earthly enemy of the Church. (332–3)

With this reasoning, Hobbes dismisses the idea that evil has a spiritual existence separate from human actions. For those who are afraid of the torments of Hell because of its supernatural quality of absolute evil, this would come as reassuring news, if they could accept it. Satan is nothing more than a metaphorical name we give to any earthly enemy of the church. We could even say that those people who are separated from God's chosen ones after the resurrection could themselves be called Satan, because they are in effect the enemies of God's sovereignty because they did not accept him in their prior lives.

After this, Hobbes provides more evidence that Hell is not as bad a place as many imagine. While one might prefer to live forever in Heaven, Hell is not a place of eternal, fiery punishment, according to Hobbes. Instead, Hell is life on earth after the resurrection, in a place separated from God and his people. A person who lives in Hell is destined, not to live forever, but to experience a 'second death' (333). 'Whereby it is evident that there is to be a second death of everyone that shall be condemned at the day of judgment, after which he shall die no more' (334).

We have to keep in mind Hobbes's overall point. He repeats in this chapter that God reigned on earth long ago, before the Jews chose kings to represent them. Jesus came to earth but proclaimed that his kingdom was not of this world. The scriptures refer to a world to come. Hobbes surmises that there are three worlds, that is, three distinct periods of time and situations of mankind: the ancient kingdom of God over the Jews, the kingdoms of earthly sovereigns, and the kingdom to come when Jesus will return to rule as an earthly sovereign himself. Presently, then, we are ruled not by God directly, but by temporal kings. Hobbes adds to this message his interpretation of the Bible on the very important subject of the afterlife, and the results are:

1. When we die, we do not go directly to Heaven or Hell, but we do not exist, our bodies only are in the ground. Therefore we should not fear immediate consequences from how we lived our lives.
2. On the day when Christ returns, there will be a general resurrection, when people will come back to life and will live a bodily existence on earth.
3. Those who have been faithful to God will live eternally on earth with Christ as king – but until that time Christ is not king, so there is no necessity for Christians to feel their loyalty divided between Christ and their earthly king.
4. Those whom God rejects will simply live out another life on earth separated from God and then die a second death. In this way, Hobbes takes some of the fear of Hell out of the equation. If, for instance, obeying your sovereign's orders was a sin after all, at least the price for that sin is not infinite.

The next chapter – following such a lengthy treatment of such an important subject as the afterlife – seems inconsequential. It is very short, and its purpose is to define 'church' according to scripture. Hobbes discusses several senses in which 'church' is used in the Bible, including as temple, as assembly of citizens, as members of a congregation, and, most significantly, as one person (that is as a legal person representing its members). This latter sense is most crucial for Hobbes because he wants to define what Church means in a Christian commonwealth. '*A Christian commonwealth and a church all one*', Hobbes begins his brief discussion, and then takes aim at the idea of any universal church which might claim dominion over many commonwealths: 'It followeth also, that there is on earth, no such universal Church, as all Christians are bound to obey; because there is no power on earth, to which all other commonwealths are subject. There are Christians, in the dominions of several princes and states; but every one of them is subject to that commonwealth, whereof he is him self a member; and consequently, cannot be subject to the commands of any other person' (340).

Here and elsewhere Hobbes is arguing against the claim of the Catholic church to be universal, to be an authority over all commonwealths and kings. Hobbes states clearly here that there is no power on earth to which independent commonwealths are subject. We know that kings are ultimately responsible to God alone, not to an earthly institution which represents God on earth. In proclaiming this, Hobbes falls into line with the policy of the English sovereign in the establishment of the Church of England, but he is also in line with the Protestant rejection of the universal church. Some Protestants would have agreed with Hobbes that the Church now falls under the authority of the state and has no universal claim to rule over earthly leaders. Others, especially the Puritans, would not exactly agree, because the acceptance or rejection of a government should be based on one's own interpretation of biblical truth. Strangely, both Catholics and Puritans claimed a higher authority as the measure for the legitimacy of earthly power. As we have already seen, Hobbes's arguments against Catholic understandings often have relevance for Puritan Protestantism as well.

Next Hobbes turns to a more thorough exposition of his comparison of the current situation and that of the ancient Israelites, establishing an even stronger connection between the ancient covenant models and his own understanding of the social contract.

This chapter is entitled 'Of the Rights of the Kingdom of God, in Abraham, Moses, the High-Priests, and the Kings of Judah'. In it, Hobbes describes how the first covenant was established by God and Abraham, through whom God ruled directly. The agreement was with Abraham and so those over whom Abraham ruled had no direct relationship with God. Instead, they were to listen to Abraham and obey his commands as the commands of God.

Hobbes continuously makes comparisons between the situation of Abraham and then Moses and contemporary sovereigns. For instance, he says that since Abraham could punish subjects who pretended to have visions and prophecy, so 'it is lawful now for the sovereign to punish any man that shall oppose his private spirit against the laws: for he hath the same place in the commonwealth, that Abraham had in his own family' (343). He asks what gave Moses authority over his people: 'His authority therefore, as the authority of all other princes, must be grounded on the consent of the people, and their promise to obey him' (344). After they made this promise (fearing direct contact with the Lord, they begged Moses to be their representative before him), they were obliged to obey Moses, just as subjects are obliged to obey their sovereign because of the social contract they have made. More directly still, Hobbes proclaims that 'we may conclude, that whosoever in a Christian commonwealth holdeth the place of Moses, is the sole messenger of God and interpreter of his commandments' (346). Further, he says that it was not the people's job to think about and interpret God's word directly – that was Moses' job. So too, it is not for the people now to interpret the scriptures for themselves or to take on any judgement in religious matters, but to listen to and respect the interpretation of their sovereign.

When God allowed rule by the priesthood to end in favour of rule over the Jews by kings, the political and religious power remained in one man. Now the priests were under the king's authority and the Bible clearly shows the kings having religious authority, even in ceremonial matters. The kings could dismiss priests and perform ceremonial religious functions themselves. So far, Hobbes has built a model by which subjects in his own commonwealth can view their monarch – as ruling by the authority of God, with sole responsibility for establishing religion within his commonwealth. But then Hobbes turns to another aspect of the history of the Israelites which does not serve as a positive example:

Nothwithstanding the government both in policy and religion, were joined, first in the high-priests, and afterwards in the kings, so far forth as concerned the right; yet it appeareth by the same holy history, that the people understood it not: but there being amongst them a great part, and probably the greatest part, that no longer than they saw great miracles, or, what is equivalent to a miracle, great abilities, or great felicity, in the enterprises of their governors, gave sufficient credit either to the fame of Moses or to the colloquies between God and the priests; they took occasion, as oft as their governors displeased them, by blaming sometimes the policy, sometimes the religion, to change the government or revolt from their obedience at their pleasure: and from thence proceeded from time to time the civil troubles, divisions, and calamities of the nation. (349)

This does not contradict Hobbes's model but rather completes it. The Israelites are not a perfect model precisely because they often did not understand their obligations as subjects. They retained the right to judge their governors and to reason about religion for themselves. Hobbes argues that whenever they did so, chaos and harm came to them. He says they 'always kept in store a pretext, either of justice or religion, to discharge themselves of their obedience, whensoever they had hope to prevail' (350). But this is precisely what the people have done in Hobbes's own country, specifically those who followed the call of the false prophets of dissenting Protestantism by revolting against their sovereign in the name of justice and religion. What we see in the history of Israel is the model of how God wants human beings to behave and relate to their governments and also how human beings often go astray.

Hobbes next turns to the role of Jesus Christ in his biblical interpretation. In this chapter (41) Christ is shown as part of the continuous relationship between God and man and part of the ongoing story of the gaining and losing and gaining again of God's kingdom. Hobbes shows how Christ's coming was foretold by the Old Testament and explains the various roles that Christ had. He explains that Christ fulfilled the role of the redeemer in a way that shows continuity with the Old Testament animal sacrifices, particularly the sacrifice of a scapegoat. God would accept this sacrifice as payment for sins and in this way Christ made himself the supreme sacrifice and redeemed mankind. Christ's second role was to '*renew the covenant of the kingdom of God, and to persuade the elect to embrace it . . .'* (354). That is, Christ's role was to restore the covenant which the Jews had rejected when they chose Saul as their king and to extend that covenant to Gentiles who would accept him. But Hobbes again makes it very clear that Christ did not intend to rule as king during his time on earth. He notes instead that Christ did not do anything to upset earthly rule: 'The kingdom he claimed was to be in another world: he taught all men to obey in the meantime them that sat in Moses' seat: he allowed them to give Cæsar his tribute, and refused to take upon himself to be a judge. How then could his words or actions be seditious, or tend to the overthrow of their then civil government?' (355).

This sentence gives us a clue to Hobbes's overall vision of Christ's role. In his view, Christ taught specifically in both word and deed exactly what Hobbes is trying to persuade his readers to accept: that until his second coming they owed their obedience to their earthly sovereigns, whose authority was sanctioned by God in a direct line of relationships, with Abraham, Moses, Aaron, the priests, and then the kings of Israel. At the present time, then, the earthly kings, such as King Charles I, are in the same position as Moses was and should be seen as having the same authority. Christ taught obedience even to imperial Rome; he did not teach that people should judge their governments. In Christ's third role, he will take up the kingship himself. But he will do this only when he returns to reign in human form on earth, as the representative of God, just as Moses had done before him: 'Again, he is to be king then, no otherwise than as subordinate or viceregent of God the Father, as Moses was in the wilderness; and as the high-priests were before the reign of Saul; and as the kings were after it' (356).

In effect, Christ will be the new Moses. Hobbes masterfully shows the continuity between the Old and New Testament and fits Christ's roles into this continuity in such a way as not to threaten the authority of earthly sovereigns. Also, even though the first two parts of *Leviathan* clearly try to establish absolute sovereignty without *reliance* upon scripture or religious reasoning, here we see Hobbes making a sort of 'divine right' argument as a *support* for his conclusions. It was not the same argument used by many other scholars to establish the divine right of kings, but it is a real attempt to show that the rule of earthly sovereigns is indeed God's will and that those sovereigns truly are God's representatives on earth for the time being. Thus, if we take these chapters in the third part of *Leviathan* seriously, we must soften the assertion of many of Hobbes's readers that he was trying to establish absolute sovereign authority with totally secular reasoning and without reference to any argument for divine sanction. Clearly he does not rely on these arguments or he would have started with them. But it would be wrong to dismiss these chapters as mere window-dressing. Hobbes believes he has shown how his theory of the social contract and absolute sovereignty fits with biblical teachings. Given much of what he has written in the first two parts, it is sometimes hard to believe that he was a serious Christian. But even if he was not, it is certain from these chapters that Hobbes was at least a serious student of the Bible and prepared to arm himself as best he could with religious reasons for his conclusions.

The next chapter (41) 'Of Power Ecclesiastical' is by far the longest chapter in *Leviathan*, which indicates the importance of this subject for Hobbes's overall scheme. This chapter lays out which powers Hobbes thinks the church and religious authorities have and do not have, using biblical proofs. First, Hobbes divides ecclesiastical history into two parts: the time before there were Christian commonwealths (before the conversion of kings), and the time when Christian commonwealths came into being. Before Christian commonwealths, ecclesiastical power was with Christ's apostles and then with others, through the laying on of hands. But what was this power? Was it the power to direct the affairs of men and make Christ's teachings law, or the power to judge whether the laws made by governments were acceptable or unacceptable to God? To these questions, Hobbes replies with a firm 'no'.

He sets up the argument he is going to make for Christian sovereigns by discussing representation. In doing so, he seems to have an unorthodox interpretation of the Christian idea of Trinity: Father, Son, and Holy Spirit. This doctrine states that there is one God, but three persons – each of which encompasses God in his entirety. Hobbes's own version of this trinitarian doctrine is that of 'personation' or representation. God, who 'has been represented, that is personated, thrice, may properly enough be said to be three persons; though neither the word Person, nor Trinity, be ascribed to him in the Bible' (360). Normally, the 'Father' part of the Trinity is not viewed as a representative, but as God in all his power. But we find that for Hobbes, even this part of the Trinity is known only through personation. He writes, 'For so God the Father, as represented by

Moses, is one person; and as represented by his Son, another person; and as represented by the apostles, and by the doctors that taught by authority from them derived, is a third person; and yet every person here, is the person of one and the same God' (360). This is obviously the view of the Trinity that made sense to Hobbes, since God himself has not been seen in all his purity. But notice that through this interpretation, there does not seem to be the same distance between Moses as God's representative, and Christ, who here is also seen as God's representative in the same way. Christians did not believe Moses or the apostles were God, but did believe that Christ was God. Hobbes does not deny that Christ was divine, but it is easy to see how this unusual interpretation of the Trinity might make other Christians confused and offended. Hobbes's purpose is not to offend, but to set up the idea of representation which can then be used to support the role of the Christian sovereign as God's modern representative. Still, the idea that a Christian sovereign might be a representative of God in any way like Christ, or even Moses, is a potentially challenging and risky one.

Hobbes's point is that '*The power ecclesiastical is but the power to teach*' (361). Christ did not leave the apostles with any governmental power, but only with the power to persuade. Hobbes quotes the Bible extensively to show that Christ taught submission to earthly authority, even if that authority was pagan. Of course, Hobbes must answer the question, what if a pagan government orders Christians to worship other gods? To answer this, Hobbes makes a distinction between inward belief and outward actions. Like so many liberal thinkers after him, he points out that no earthly power can enforce internal belief, only outward behaviour. A person can believe in Christ despite every order of his pagan government. But what if a person is told to act in defiance of Christian commandments? Hobbes's answer is that if he is doing so by direct order of his sovereign, then the moral responsibility lies with the sovereign and not with his subjects, who are simply obeying as they are told to do in the Bible.

What about the admiration for martyrs in the Christian tradition, those who died at the hands of their lawful governments rather than act against their faith? It would appear from many Bible stories that resisting the government in faithfulness to God's commands is a virtue. Here Hobbes performs a manoeuvre of definition which he hopes will alleviate the issue of martyrdom:

But what then shall we say of all those martyrs we read of in the history of the Church, that they have needlessly cast away their lives? For answer hereunto, we are to distinguish the persons that have been for that cause put to death: whereof some have received a calling to preach, and profess the kingdom of Christ openly; others have had no such calling, nor more has been required of them than their own faith. The former sort, if they have been put to death, for bearing witness to this point, that Jesus Christ is risen from the dead, were true martyrs; for a martyr is, (to give the true definition of the word) a witness of the resurrection of Jesus the Messiah; which none can be but those that conversed with him on earth, and saw him after he was risen: for a witness must have seen what he testifieth, or else his testimony is not good. (365)

Notice that Hobbes has accomplished at least two things already that work to the advantage of his overall theory. First, he defines 'martyr' as someone who bears witness to Christ's resurrection, not, as commonly thought, someone who dies for his beliefs. It may seem that he ties martyrdom with being put to death, but when he actually gives the definition, it is simply 'a witness of the resurrection of Jesus the Messiah'. Second, he construes 'witness' very narrowly, to include only those who actually saw Christ during the time in which he lived on earth. As he says a little further on, it must be 'some disciple that conversed with him, and saw him before and after the resurrection; and consequently must be one of his original disciples: whereas they which were not so, can witness no more but that their antecessors said it, and are therefore but witnesses of other men's testimony; and are but second martyrs, or martyrs of Christ's witnesses' (365). Through these redefinitions, Hobbes accomplishes two more things: he teaches people that they do not have to die for their faith, and he also teaches that they cannot be martyrs by 'witnessing' today. Only people who saw Christ in the flesh could truly be witnesses. To make his point and purpose even more clear, Hobbes says 'To die for every tenet that serveth the ambition or profit of the clergy, is not required; nor is it the death of the witness, but the testimony itself that makes the martyr: for the word signifieth nothing else, but the man that beareth witness, whether he be put to death for his testimony or not' (366).

Some parts of this chapter take special aim at the Catholic church and its claims to spiritual and temporal authority. For instance, Hobbes discusses the church's power to forgive or retain sins.

Through an examination of Bible passages, Hobbes argues first that the apostles could not refuse to forgive those who were truly repentant, and second that the judgement concerning whether a person was repentant did not belong to the apostles, but to the whole Christian community. He indicates that, after Christian commonwealths were instituted, the representative of the commonwealth would have this power of judgement.

Likewise, Hobbes deals with the power of the church to excommunicate its members. Excommunication to most people meant the church's power to deny its members the sacraments, especially the Eucharist, or communion. For Roman Catholics, it meant being separated from the forgiveness and love of Christ, and therefore damnation. First, Hobbes defines excommunication as simply the members of the church shunning or not including someone. Next, he determines that 'excommunication, in the time that Christian religion was not authorized by the civil power, was used only for a correction of manners, not of errors in opinion: for it is a punishment, whereof none could be sensible but such as believed, and expected the coming again of our Saviour to judge the world; and they who so believed, needed no other opinion, but uprightness of life, to be saved' (371).

In other words, excommunication would have no effect on a nonbeliever, who would not be afraid of being cut off from the Church's benefits. So excommunication must be something reserved only for those who believe, but whose misbehaviour sets them apart from the Christian community. Hobbes makes this clear when he says that 'to excommunicate a man that held this foundation, that Jesus was the Christ, for difference of opinion in other points, by which that foundation was not destroyed, there appeareth no authority in the Scripture, nor example in the apostles' (371). So, for instance, if the Catholic church threatens to excommunicate those converted to Protestantism, or a king who divorces his wife, it is the church that is wrong to do so as long as the citizens or king still believe that Jesus is the Christ. Therefore, a believing Christian should not disobey his sovereign for fear of excommunication. Excommunication of such a person, Hobbes argues, has no effect. Indeed, during the time of Christian commonwealths, if excommunication does not have the authority of the civil sovereign, it is meaningless.

Much of this chapter supports Hobbes's view of the king of the Christian commonwealth as the chief pastor. Hobbes discusses his view of how religious truth was determined in the time of the apostles, up until the time of Christian commonwealths. In the past, truth was determined through a process of group deliberation. No one was prohibited from reading and interpreting the scriptures for himself. Echoing the idea of philosopher-kings in Plato's *Republic*, Hobbes says, 'And as it was in the apostle's time, it must be till such time as there should be pastors, that could authorize an interpreter whose interpretation should generally be stood to: but that could not be till kings were pastors, or pastors kings' (376). Plato taught that there could be no perfect justice unless philosophers became kings, which he thought was almost impossible. For Plato, the possibility of wise leadership was remote because 1) the wise would not want to rule, and 2) the people would not accept the leadership of their intellectual superiors. Apparently, in Hobbes's view, the pastor-king is more feasible and acceptable to the people than the philosopher-king. Perhaps this is because the king's authority rests on the people's self-interest and religiosity, as well as his own power, rather than on the people's estimation of his intellectual gifts.

Also an argument for the Christian sovereign's authority is Hobbes's treatment of the Ten Commandments. Who gave these Commandments the force of law, asks Hobbes. The answer is Moses, of course, who ruled as God's representative and held the civil power over Israel. Through the people's consent, Moses could make the commandments the law of the land. The same power belonged to Aaron and his successors as civil sovereigns. Hobbes gives the sovereigns of his day the same power: the Ten Commandments become law only as the civil sovereign interprets them. Remember that Hobbes equated much of the natural law with God's law. He is saying the same thing here as he did in Part I of *Leviathan*: nothing has the force of law until the sovereign makes it so. Otherwise others could dispute the sovereign's interpretation of God's law.

Hobbes continues to try to separate the church's offices and functions, such as the office of bishops and ministers, or the functions of teaching and guiding, from any sort of official church authority. This is to show that the church originally had no power over people except the power of persuasion and that there was no special political power placed in the church's officials, as the Catholic church claimed. Hobbes argues that the early practices of the church were much more consensual and democratic than those of the Catholic church of his day, casting further doubt on separate ecclesiastical authority. Hobbes reiterates that with the advent of Christian sovereigns, the authority to do things like establish tithes (mandatory contributions), or make church appointments, and even to determine church teachings, falls to the sovereign as the 'supreme pastor' (393). 'The *pastoral authority of sovereigns only is* jure divino: *that of other pastors is* jure civili' (394). Only the sovereign's authority comes from God, whereas all other pastors' authority comes from the sovereign. To make this relationship perfectly clear when it comes to the Catholic church, Hobbes writes: 'If they [Christian sovereigns] please, therefore, they may, as many Christian kings now do, commit the government of their subjects in matters of religion to the Pope; but then the Pope is in that point subordinate to them, and exerciseth that charge in another's dominion jure civili, in the right of the civil sovereign; not jure divino, in God's right; and may therefore be discharged of that office, when the sovereign, for the good of his subjects, shall think it necessary' (398–9).

Near the end of the chapter, for good measure, Hobbes takes on Cardinal Bellarmine's arguments in his *Summo Pontifice* for the separate and superior authority of the pope. Hobbes interprets some of the chief biblical passages that might support the special status and authority of the Church of Rome in ways that clearly undermine that support. Famously, Hobbes writes: 'Men cannot serve two masters. They ought therefore to ease them, either by holding the reins of government wholly in their own hands; or by wholly delivering them into the hands of the Pope; that such men as are willing to be obedient, may be protected in their obedience. For this distinction of temporal and spiritual power is but words. Power is as really divided, and as dangerously to all purposes, by sharing with another *indirect* power, as with a *direct* one' (417).

This helps clear up any confusion. Even though Hobbes works to separate the church's spiritual teachings from any temporal authority, he is certainly not working to separate church and state. It is wrong to ask men to 'serve two masters', to choose whom to obey on any given issue. There can be no sharing of power, or giving to the church an indirect power over spiritual matters, without risking dangerous divisions. Again, Hobbes reminds his readers that the real danger is civil war – the dissolution of government. Therefore, either keep all authority lodged in the sovereign, or give it all to the pope. Since the Catholic church continued to claim an independent authority at least over spiritual matters and often over temporal matters as well, Hobbes is arguing that those sovereigns who choose to allow the pope to be the spiritual leader of the people are tempting fate. They are risking their own authority and the safety of their people. In the end, Hobbes makes it clear that even if the civil sovereign is considered an infidel or heretic by the pope or by his own subjects, those subjects still owe him complete obedience. It simply is not up to the church or the people to judge the sovereign in any way – only God can judge the sovereign. As Orwin puts it, 'Man can serve two masters after all. In serving his sovereign he is serving his God; yet at the same time the service of his God, requiring as it does no manifestations but this one, cannot impede his service to the sovereign' (Orwin 1975: 38).

The final chapter in this third part of *Leviathan* is chapter 43, 'Of What is Necessary for a Man's Reception into the Kingdom of Heaven'. Here Hobbes takes up again the very real fear people had of the punishments of Hell. What must they do, who must they obey, to make sure that they do not go to Hell? First, Hobbes argues for the importance of intention, an inner quality which may not match external behaviour. The obedience required by God, he writes, 'is a serious endeavour to obey him', because God 'accepteth in all our actions the will for the deed . . .' (425). Since, as we know, our intentions and internal beliefs are free from coercion, it is possible to obey God completely by this criterion, even if in our actions we obey an infidel king. Hobbes further emphasizes the importance of internal belief when he explains that there is only one necessary article of faith which one must believe internally in order to be assured of Heaven: 'The, *unum necessarium*, only article of faith, which the Scripture maketh simply necessary to salvation, is this, that JESUS IS THE CHRIST' (428). Hobbes provides various arguments, scriptural and logical, to back this up, but the most characteristically Hobbesian is this: 'For if an inward assent of the mind to all the doctrines concerning Christian faith now taught, whereof the greatest part are disputed, were necessary to salvation, there would be nothing in the world so hard as to be a Christian' (429–30).

So the only obedience demanded by God is the internal desire and intention to obey, and the only faith necessary is the belief that Jesus is the Christ. Neither of these requirements demand any outward action. So, if the sovereign is either an infidel, or a Christian who nevertheless commands unsound beliefs and practices in his subjects, the subjects are still spiritually safe, protected from Hell so long as they intend to obey God and believe that Jesus is Christ. There is no duty to proclaim one's belief or to act on it in any way, if the sovereign commands otherwise. Indeed, as we have seen, there is a Christian duty to obey the sovereign, even in these matters. The responsibility, as Hobbes has argued elsewhere, lies squarely with the sovereign, who will someday have to face God.

### Questions

1. Hobbes spends more time casting doubt in this section on the validity of prophecy, spirits, miracles, biblical authorship, and inspiration. Why?
2. What is Hobbes's main purpose in addressing biblical teachings in this section? Do you agree that Hobbes's use of the Bible is merely rhetorical, or do you think he is making a genuine effort to understand the Bible?
3. How does Hobbes define the 'Kingdom of God', and Heaven and Hell? What political importance may these definitions have?
4. What must a Christian do to be saved and go to Heaven, according to Hobbes? What is the political importance of this teaching?

### PART IV: OF THE KINGDOM OF DARKNESS

This part of *Leviathan* is relatively short, with only four chapters. But the subject is quite interesting, dealing at first with subjects like 'spiritual darkness', and 'demonology', and then quite amusingly with various errors Hobbes believes result from ancient philosophy and medieval theology. It can also be quite offensive, dealing very critically with cherished religious beliefs. Why is Hobbes writing about these subjects (or should we say, writing about them again in a more thorough and forceful way)? As we get into these chapters we will quickly realize that a large part of Hobbes's agenda here is to launch a more sustained assault (already more than hinted at elsewhere in the book) on the Roman Catholic church.[18]

It is clear that Hobbes is much closer to the Protestant understanding of many Christian doctrines, although his understanding is also in many ways unique. Arguments that have been covered by Hobbes earlier need not be dealt with in detail again. Instead, we will focus on what is unique in these chapters and what they add to

Hobbes's previous arguments. By attacking supernaturalism in a politically acceptable way, through criticism of various Catholic beliefs and practices, Hobbes once again provides a profound challenge to anyone who believes in anything that does not arise from nature in the usual (non-supernatural, non-miraculous) way.

As Benjamin Milner points out, Hobbes's 'immanentistic theology cannot really support biblical religion, for, as we have seen, it entails a thoroughly naturalistic understanding of religious phenomena, phenomena that, in the biblical and orthodox view of things, require a supernatural foundation' (Milner 1988: 415). So even though he appears to be simply assaulting Catholic beliefs, taken in the context of his overall treatment of religion in *Leviathan*, we can see here the substance of an attack on any religious beliefs that stray beyond an understanding of what Hobbes calls 'natural religion'. While Catholicism might have called for more belief in the manifestly supernatural or miraculous, as Milner and others point out, Protestantantism also demanded a belief in the supernatural ability of God to work miracles not of an outward nature but of an inward, spiritual nature.[19]

Hobbes starts chapter 44, 'Of Spiritual Darkness, from Misinterpretation of Scripture', with an immediate rationalizing of a fearful belief, among most Christians, of Satan and Hell. He invokes the names Satan and Beelzebub, then defines Beelzebub as 'prince of phantasms . . .' (437). So far he sounds like he believes in these spiritual entities. But we know from what he has already written in previous sections that this is unlikely and indeed he rather quickly turns to a rationalization. The kingdom of darkness over which Satan rules is really 'nothing else but a *confederacy of deceivers, that to obtain dominion over men in this present world, endeavour by dark and erroneous doctrines, to extinguish in them the light, both of nature, and of the gospel; and so to disprepare them for the kingdom of God to come*' (437). This confederacy of deceivers consists not of supernatural beings but of men and in particular the leadership of the Catholic church. Hobbes turns to a discussion of the four causes of spiritual darkness, all of which point most directly to the teachings of that church. In this chapter, he chooses to elaborate on the first cause, which is the misinterpretation of the scriptures or 'the abuse of Scripture' (438).

Hobbes claims that the greatest abuse of the scriptures is to read them as supporting the idea that the kingdom of God is present in the world today (when we know that Hobbes thinks it was dissolved at the time that the Jews asked Saul to be their king), and that this kingdom is the church and the pope is its 'vicar' or leader (Milner 1988: 416–17). This claim leads, as we know, to further claims that challenge sovereign authority and which lead to violence and disorder. Hobbes next turns to an abuse of the scripture that seems to be uniquely Catholic: '*mistaking consecration for conjuration*' or a magical spell (441). Consecration, he argues, is using words to separate out ordinary things for a holy or sacred use, but 'when by such words, the nature or quality of the thing itself, is pretended to be changed, it is not consecration, but either an extraordinary work of God, or a vain and impious conjuration. But seeing, for the frequency of pretending the change of nature in their consecrations, it cannot be esteemed a work extraordinary, it is no other than a conjuration or incantation, whereby they would have men to believe an alteration of nature that is not, contrary to the testimony of man's sight, and of all the rest of his senses' (442).

So Hobbes distinguishes between using words to signify the special use of something, as opposed to using words to, in his view, cast a magical spell which changes the substance of a thing. All Christians of Hobbes's day, Protestant and Catholic, would have agreed that magic was a dark art and had nothing to do with God or his works. However, Protestants accused Catholics of believing in magic, and worse, committing the sin of idolatry, which Hobbes presently mentions. On the other hand, Catholics thought that what they believed in was not magic but the actual workings of God through the actions of the priests and the church. What Hobbes is mainly aiming at in the passage above is the Catholic belief in transubstantiation. Hobbes sees this as priestly deception, the claiming of magical powers by the priests to keep the people in awe.

Protestants saw communion in a different way than Catholics, but they disagreed on the issue of exactly what was going on – from believing that Christ's spirit was infused in the elements to believing that the Lord's supper was a commemorative re-enactment of Christ's last supper. So Hobbes, like the most radical Protestant, mocks the Catholic idea that the substance of the bread and wine change, even though the outward appearance is the same, even going so for as to state bluntly that it is a form of 'lying' and 'gross idolatry' (442). But given Hobbes's treatment of spiritual things, we can reasonably surmise that he would disagree with Lutheran and Calvinist Protestants and any others who thought that somehow Christ's spirit, at least, was there. For him, communion can only be a commemorative event. Hobbes likewise criticizes the Catholic use of holy water, baptism and exorcism. In the Catholic baptism ceremony there is an initial exorcism of the infant to ensure its spiritual well-being. Hobbes can almost be heard laughing when he writes, 'As if all children, till blown on by the priest, were demoniacs' (443).

One uniquely Catholic doctrine that Hobbes spends quite a bit of time refuting is the idea of Purgatory, that place of punishment for sins before a person goes to Heaven. For this and other beliefs, he partly blames the teachings of the Greeks (and the church's embracing of those teachings through its medieval scholarship). It was the Greeks who taught:

> That the souls of men were substances distinct from their bodies, and therefore that when the body was dead, the soul of every man, whether godly or wicked, must subsist somewhere by virtue of its own nature, without acknowledging therein any supernatural gift of God; the doctors of the Church doubted a long time, what was the place, which they were to abide in, till they should be reunited to their bodies in the resurrection; supposing for a while, they lay under altars; but afterward the Church of Rome found it more profitable to build for them this place of purgatory; which by some other Churches in this latter age has been demolished. (445–6)

In this passage, Hobbes historicizes the church's teachings on Purgatory – church leaders came up with the idea after lengthy reflection, so it was a teaching of the church not a teaching of Christ with any real biblical foundation. In this way, he casts suspicion on the motives of church fathers and the scholars who expounded the idea. Indeed, further on in the chapter he shows how the belief that time in Purgatory could be reduced by the prayers of those still on earth, prayers of the saints, and indulgences (grants of forgiveness from the church) led to abuses of church power. Since the corruption of the church which Luther protested against (including the sale of indulgences) was still very much in the Protestant mind, Hobbes is on firm political ground criticizing the whole idea of Purgatory. He rails at length against Purgatory (and Cardinal Bellarmine, a contemporary apologist for Catholicism, who claimed biblical evidence of it).[20] This is precisely because it puts so much fear into people's hearts that they will obey the church rather than their sovereign, thinking more of the priest's power to relieve their time in Purgatory than in the power of the king.[21] Hobbes reasserts in this chapter that when people die, their souls do not live on (let alone go to Purgatory). The soul is really just the animating force and it dies with the body. God will, according to Christian faith, raise all people back to life at the second coming of Christ and, as we know, the righteous will live eternally on earth, while the unrighteous will simply die a second death.[22]

The central purpose of the next chapter (45) is to link many of the practices which Hobbes thinks are superstitious and politically dangerous to the much-maligned ancient pagans. This time he does not target the ancient philosophers and historians, but instead the ancient peoples themselves in their religions, traditions, and cultural practices. This chapter is entitled 'Demonology, and other Relics of the Religion of the Gentiles'. Hobbes begins, one might like to say, back at the very beginning in Part I, 'Of Man', where he discusses what produces sight and what makes men see things that are not there. This is the origin of 'demonology' or belief in spirits. Because people's sight is actually an internal faculty and therefore what we see is not always produced by external stimuli, people believe in ghosts and spirits. But what people believe are ghosts and spirits are really phantasms, dreams, and nightmares. Because people in the past could not explain what they 'saw', they created the idea of demons (a word they used to mean both good and evil spirits) and this idea spread to the Jews. Christian converts, moreover, continued to believe in these demons and other pagan ideas as we will see, despite their conversions. For Hobbes, of course, there is no truth to these beliefs. He states here as elsewhere that ancient people called demonic possession what his contemporaries would call 'lunacy' or what we might, in even more enlightened times, call mental illness. He goes again through the arguments he uses elsewhere to show that when the Bible mentions demons possessing people or Christ driving demons out, or of Satan tempting Christ, it means these things *figuratively*. Hobbes insists that nowhere in the Bible can it really be proven that demons or Satan are spiritual entities separable from the people involved. When Christ ordered demons out of people, he was simply using the vernacular of the day in order to be understood. When Hobbes asks the obvious question of why Christ would not have made an effort to clear up this confusion so that people did not believe in demons, Hobbes retreats into piety: 'But if there be no immaterial spirit, or any possession of men's bodies by any spirit corporeal, it may again be asked, why our Saviour and his apostles did not teach the people so; and in such clear words, as they might no more doubt thereof. But such questions as these, are more curious, than necessary for a Christian man's salvation. Men may as well ask why Christ, that could have given to all men faith, piety, and all manner of moral virtues, gave it to some only, and not to all . . .' (464–5).

In other words, some things must remain a mystery!

Hobbes next turns back to idol worship, reiterating his definition of worship and distinguishing civil from religious worship. He defines idolatry as worshiping God, who is seen as inhabiting some object that is made by man (and not ordered made by God, to get around the few exceptions in the Bible, such as the Ark of the Covenant). While this might seem like a fairly uncontroversial definition of idolatry, Hobbes's discussion again takes a critical turn in the direction of Catholicism as he returns to a treatment of the Eucharist or Holy Communion. Hobbes refers to the pious practice of Catholics of adoring or worshipping the Eucharist because of their belief that it is the actual body and blood of Christ. Here again he agrees with the Protestant charge that the scriptural passage 'this is my body' should not be read literally, but figuratively, as 'this represents my body'. The Catholic church is thus encouraging the faithful to commit idolatry when encouraging them to adore the host. Again, Hobbes's concern is social and political: if people believe that there is an institution which can literally bring Christ into the world in religious worship, who could argue that it, and not the sovereign power, is the more awesome institution?

Hobbes then distinguishes between idolatrous worship and 'scandalous worship of images'. A 'scandal' in this sense means something that encourages people to sin. Hobbes suggests the example of a pagan king who orders the worship of an idol. Are Christians guilty of sin for worshipping it? We would suspect not, given what he has said earlier in similar discussions – Hobbes has elsewhere argued that any sin must lie with the sovereign, since it is the subject's whole duty to obey. Here, however, he makes a distinction between pastors and laity. While a common man can apparently worship the idol without sin if he detests it in his heart, and is not guilty of scandalizing his fellow subjects even if they follow him, apparently the authority figure (the pastor) is guilty of the sin of scandalizing his fellow Christians if he does the same: 'If therefore a pastor lawfully called to teach and direct others, or any other, of whose knowledge there is a great opinion, do external honour to an idol for fear; unless he make his fear and unwillingness to it, as evident as the worship; he scandalizeth his brother, by seeming to approve idolatry' (472).

The reader is left to wonder exactly how Hobbes can make this distinction and place the responsibility on the pastor not to lead his flock astray, even when he is in fear of death – which fear Hobbes has repeatedly asserted excuses all actions. It is important to note that Hobbes is discussing pastors 'lawfully called to teach and direct others'. If they are lawfully called upon to teach others, this must be because the sovereign has appointed them to do it. So doesn't their duty consist in obeying the sovereign in all things, even in idolatry? Or, if the pastor has fallen under the control of a rival kingdom or other party which is threatening him with death, would not Hobbes normally say that his allegiance to his previous sovereign is dissolved and that he should, for fear of death, obey his new sovereign? A little later, Hobbes says that such a pastor has committed a sin, which does not seem to agree with his previous teaching. He does, however, say that the pastor can absolve himself of this sin if he makes his fear and unwillingness to worship known to all so that others will not be encouraged to follow him – but how can the pastor do this without disobeying the sovereign and risking his life? Suffice it to say that this is one of the more mysterious passages in *Leviathian*, by a philosopher known for his consistency, and bears more study.

Hobbes next ties worship of saints, images, and relics to the ancients, arguing that the Catholic church still allows or even encourages such things that are leftovers from the pagan past. He theorizes that the church, not wanting to alienate new converts, allowed pagan idols to be kept in the homes of new Christians. Statues of Venus and Cupid became statues of the Virgin Mary and the Christ Child. He claims that canonization of saints actually started in ancient Rome with the proclamation, after their deaths, that the emperors were in heaven, looking down with favour upon the city. Even Catholic religious processions – the use of candles and many holidays – are in Hobbes's view derived from the pagan past. All of this is pointed out to identify the Roman Catholic church with paganism and, by inference, is praise of those brands of Protestantism which are the most rational and least supernatural or superstitious in his view.[23]

In Chapter 46, 'Of Darkness from Vain Philosophy, and Fabulous Tradition', Hobbes is most concerned to expose how the 'philosophy' embraced by the church has led to what he considers distortions and errors in modern thought. He starts with his own definition of philosophy, and then goes on to argue that what others call 'philosophy' is no such thing: '*By PHILOSOPHY is understood the knowledge acquired by reasoning, from the manner of the generation of any thing, to the properties; or from the properties, to some possible way of generation of the same; to the end to be able to produce, as far as matter, and human force permit, such effects, as human life requireth.*'

So philosophy is either inductive or deductive reasoning for a practical end – to produce things people need to live. Of course, these things are not just items like food, clothing and shelter, but also peace and security. We can see that for Hobbes, philosophy is very goal-oriented and practical. It is not about speculation and conjecture, but the gathering of facts and reasoning about them. Hobbes features geometry as the pre-eminent science because it starts with clear, agreed-upon definitions and explanations and generates usable theorems that can solve real-world problems. So much of what passed for science in ancient times, or in his own day, is considered by Hobbes to be vanity and fantasy.

First, and keeping always in mind the bad example of the church and its scholars, Hobbes separates true philosophy from supernatural revelation and knowledge based merely on authority and tradition. He rather sensibly points out that philosophy cannot really start until people have achieved the level of civilization that brings leisure to allow them time to think. This makes the establishment of the secure commonwealth a prerequisite for social and economic advancement. Hobbes briefly covers the development of the ancient Greek and Roman philosophies of Plato, Aristotle, the Stoics, and the Jews. He concludes that all of these past schools of thought have been 'unprofitable'. That is, judging by what they have produced, these schools have proved themselves to be unsound. We already know that Hobbes attributes much of the disorder of his own day to the teachings about human liberty and democratic government supposedly advanced by the ancients, especially Aristotle, and then carried forward into his world by church scholars. Hobbes's hostility to the ancient philosophers can be explained when we understand that many Catholic doctrines were developed in the light of Neo-Platonism and Aristotelian thought. Even Jewish philosophy was tainted by Plato and Aristotle. Here Hobbes goes to greater lengths to expose the logical errors of these ways of thinking.

The ancients had ideas such as 'forms' or ideals which could not be seen but nevertheless were considered to exist in greater perfection than actual visible things.[24] Also, the ancients formulated the idea of the human soul as a separate entity and separable from the human body, an idea with which we know Hobbes disagrees. In the same manner, theologians of the past and Hobbes's present talked about souls or spirits as 'abstract essences' having no material existence but being nonetheless real. Words such as *'essence, essential, essentiality'* (484) and the like were used by scholars to imply something more pure and separable from mundane existence. But Hobbes, ever the materialist, rejects the use of such words as nonsense.

If the reader is wondering why Hobbes is so concerned about the use of words in scholarly speculations, it is because he believes they have real, and entirely negative, consequences. Hobbes ties them to church teachings which lead to fear of ghosts and devils, transubstantiation, inspiration, souls' existence in Purgatory, and even the idea of the Trinity, as 'magical' things which make people fear and respect the power of the church more than their government. These beliefs, which Hobbes clearly identifies as superstition, originate in the ancient idea that non-material things can exist separately from the material world they nonetheless inhabit.

Hobbes cleverly, and with good humour, runs through some examples of how the 'logic' or 'reasoning' of the ancients and of Catholic theologians is really simply circular: 'The Schools will tell you out of Aristotle, that the bodies that sink downwards, are *heavy*; and that this *heaviness* is it that causes them to descend. But if you ask what they mean by heaviness, they will define it to be an endeavour to go to the centre of the earth. So that the cause why things sink downward, is an endeavour to be below: which is as much as to say, that bodies descend, or ascend, because they do' (487).

Circular reasoning such as this is no reasoning at all. Rather, in Hobbes's view, it is a way to confirm, through mysterious and seemingly authoritative language, what you already think to be true. Such language, in his view, is most often used to obtain the consent of simpler men who will think that there is more reasoning going on, especially if plenty of 'jargon' is used. In Hobbes's view, it is better to find out what we can with real philosophy and to admit that some things, especially having to do with the nature of God, are 'incomprehensible' (488).

Much of the rest of this chapter covers territory we are now familiar with – the idea that the ancients and the church have developed ways of thinking that encourage individual or priestly judgement of government and thus do not help keep the proper relationship between individuals, the church, and the state. There is one point that he makes, however, that can aid us in seeing the nascent 'liberal' element in Hobbes's thought, and which we could occasionally glimpse earlier, especially in Part II of *Leviathan*. Hobbes objects to the church's attempt to rule even the person's interior conscience. He even brings in the word 'inquisition' and the situation in which 'men are either punished for answering the truth of their thoughts, or constrained to answer an untruth for fear of punishment' (491). In a clear demarcation of what the church or government can enforce and what it cannot, Hobbes writes: 'It is true, that the civil magistrate, intending to employ a minister in the charge of teaching, may enquire of him, if he be content to preach such and such doctrines; and in case of refusal, may deny him the employment. But to force him to accuse himself of opinions, when his actions are not by law forbidden, is against the law of nature; and especially in them, who teach, that a man shall be damned to eternal and extreme torments if he die in a false opinion concerning an article of the Christian faith' (491).

Of course, Hobbes is aiming at the medieval church's practices, especially the Inquisition and its attempts to control people's thoughts as well as their actions. But notice that what he says is applied here to the 'civil magistrate' and not just to church authorities. If a man refuses to teach the doctrines the civil authority wants him to teach, he can be fired. But certainly, there are places in *Leviathan* where it would seem that the magistrate is within his rights to have the man arrested for refusing. A little further into this passage, Hobbes does make it clear that the man is free to refuse only if his actions are not forbidden by law. So, if the sovereign is inclined to make it a law to force people to teach what they do not believe, then the man could be arrested. But here, Hobbes ties the issue up with interior conscience and the idea that we cannot be forced to believe anything we don't want to believe. He even invokes the 'law of nature' in defence of interior freedom. The thrust of this passage is on the side of free thought (though not free actions), especially, as he points out, because Christians hold that false beliefs can lead to damnation. At the end of this chapter, Hobbes makes some similar points, condemning the church for its suppression of philosophical/ scientific thought. He seems here to be a champion for the development of truth, though he does qualify this with his confirmation that the civil sovereign can outlaw even the advancement of scientific truth – but it should be the civil sovereign that does so, not the church. In Hobbes's view, as we know, the civil sovereign has a good reason to allow science and philosophy to develop freely. The intelligent sovereign wants to advance prosperity and civilization, whereas in Hobbes's view the church would lose much authority by allowing some of its truths to be exposed as antagonistic to scientific reason. Some aspects of Hobbes's reasoning in these passages are not that far removed from the arguments in John Locke's *Letter Concerning Toleration*.

In the final chapter (47) of this fourth part of *Leviathan*, Hobbes asks the question '*cui bono?*', or who benefits from all of the false teachings he has discussed in the previous three chapters. Hobbes reasons that a person can often find the original source of a teaching by asking this question. Of course, the most obvious answer is the Roman Catholic church, which is empowered by all of these teachings. To make this answer abundantly clear, Hobbes goes to some lengths to compare the Roman church to the kingdom of the fairies or old wives' tales. But the less obvious but still quite clear answer is that the Presbyterian Protestants also benefit from some of the same teachings. This linking of the Presbyterians, heavily responsible in Hobbes's view for the recent civil war in his own country, with the problems the Catholic church had caused, was about the worst insult that Hobbes could throw at Presbyterians. After all, the Presbyterians thought that their doctrine was the absolute opposite of Roman Catholic corruption. But Hobbes finds some rather fundamental ways in which their claims overlap. The most important is mentioned fairly early on in this chapter: 'But in those places where the presbytery took the office, though many other doctrines of the Church of Rome were forbidden to be taught; yet this doctrine, that the kingdom of Christ is already come, and that it began at the resurrection of our Saviour, was still retained. But *cui bono?*' (495).

We know that this doctrine of the immanence of the kingdom of God is one that Hobbes has thoroughly refuted because he deems it extremely dangerous to public authority. If the kingdom of God is immanent, it must be represented somewhere. Whoever that representative is will necessarily have a strong claim to power. Even though the Presbyterians did not make claims such as infallibility of leadership or the apostolic succession of any pope-like figure, in Hobbes's view they still made claims to represent Christ's will in the world. In effect, they made the same kind of claim for themselves that the authorities of the Catholic church also made. So adamant is Hobbes about this accusation against the Presbyterians that he ends this chapter and indeed his book (except his 'Review and Conclusion') with the following reminder: 'But who knows that this spirit of Rome, now gone out, and walking by missions through the dry places of China, Japan, and the Indies, that yield him little fruit, may not return, or rather an assembly of spirits worse than he, enter, and inhabit this clean swept house, and make the end thereof worse than the beginning? For it is not the Roman clergy only, that pretends the kingdom of God to be of this world, and thereby to have a power therein, distinct from that of the civil state' (502).

This appears in the very last paragraph of this last chapter of Part IV. Hobbes places so much emphasis on it that it can be taken as indicating the purpose of his writing about the Kingdom of Darkness as a whole: to warn his readers in England and elsewhere that the Catholic church is not the only religious institution which threatens with claims to spiritual authority to take power away from lawful sovereigns. The Presbyterians were and are such a threat in his view, and so is anyone else who makes claims to speak for God other than the civil sovereign and those whom he appoints. Hobbes clearly blames rulers who, in the past, have allowed the clergy to become presumptuous and encroach upon royal power. So, his book serves as a thorough warning to those who, in the future, do not watch closely over the religious leaders within their dominions.

Also in this final chapter, Hobbes describes the loosening of three 'knots' that have bound England politically and spiritually and which have all been untied. The first knot, the rule of the Roman church, was cut by King Henry VIII, and ties were further weakened by Queen Elizabeth, who also tried to root out the Catholic influence in her country. The second knot, the authority of the Anglican bishops, was cut by the Presbyterians whose revolt brought down the monarchy and made Presbyterianism the religion of the land. The third knot, the rule of the Presbyterians, was subsequently cut by their political collapse.

In discussing the third knot, Hobbes is probably referring here to the takeover of parliament by Oliver Cromwell in 1648, in which many members of parliament who wished to accept an accommodation with Charles I were ejected. This left the more radical Protestant elements in charge, which led to the execution of Charles I and the establishment of a Commonwealth without a monarch. In response to the latter development, Hobbes writes 'we are reduced to the independency of the primitive Christians, to follow Paul, or Cephas, or Apollos, every man as he liketh best . . .' (499). This independence, Hobbes says, 'is perhaps the best' (499). Coming from a man who has held that spiritual independence is dangerous, this latter comment is strange. And this is compounded by a further explanation:

> First, because there ought to be no power over the consciences of men, but of the Word itself, working faith in every one, not always according to the purpose of them that plant and water, but of God himself, that giveth the increase. And secondly, because it is unreasonable in them, who teach there is such danger in every little error, to require of a man endued with reason of his own, to follow the reason of any other man, or of the most voices of any other men, which is little better than to venture his salvation at cross and pile. (499)

What does Hobbes have in mind by making this argument, especially at this point in his book? Again, these statements sound very similar to those made by Locke in his *Letter Concerning Toleration* (1963 [1689]), though unlike Locke, Hobbes certainly does not go on to argue for toleration. Doesn't Hobbes think that individual independence in matters religious leads to chaos? Yes, but if we look at this rather enlightened statement within the context of Hobbes's overall teachings concerning the value of establishment and the purpose and limits of religious institutions, we can perhaps see more clearly how this statement might make sense. Perhaps we can at least say that Hobbes would prefer an established church that demands outward conformity but which does not attempt to delve into and control the hearts of men, a church that allows people to hear and benefit from the Word of God (rightly understood) but does not strain people's patience by demanding continual oaths. After all, Hobbes wants a Christian religion which is more like a civil religion, a religion that primarily functions to support the sovereign, promoting peace and tranquillity. Hobbes knows that too much coercion in religious matters can have the opposite effect and tempt men (even though they should not be tempted) to rebel.

## Questions

1. Hobbes attacked the Roman Catholic church in Part III, and he does so even more in this part of *Leviathan*. How do his attacks on Catholic teachings undermine many Protestant religious beliefs as well? What was Hobbes's purpose in doing this?
2. Explain how Hobbes ties together the ancient philosophers and the teaching of the Catholic church. What is wrong with this relationship between ancient philosophy and church theology?
3. What criticisms of Presbyterians does Hobbes make in this section? How does he tie them together with his criticisms of the Catholic church, and why?

## HOBBES'S REVIEW AND CONCLUSION

Hobbes uses a brief final section, 'A Review, and Conclusion', to tie up loose ends in his arguments and to assert his purpose once more. He starts out, however, by observing that to persuade people, both reason and rhetoric are needed: 'Again, in all deliberations, and in all pleadings, the faculty of solid reasoning is necessary: for without it, the resolutions of men are rash, and their sentences unjust: and yet if there be not powerful eloquence, which procureth attention and consent, the effect of reason will be little' (503).

By saying this, Hobbes acknowledges once again that human nature is reasonable but also passionate. To persuade people, one must appeal to their emotions and not just their reason. Certainly this is true with a large political project such as Hobbes is proposing. Hobbes wants his theory taught in universities and preached from pulpits. He wants monarchs to understand it and teach it through what they say and do. Hobbes's theory cannot, and it has not, been a dry and boring scientific treatise with no passion or blood. Hobbes would not have bothered to spend so many pages of ink on supplying biblical support for his views, or much time criticizing the rash gentry, educated men, Presbyterians or Catholics so harshly and sometimes humorously if he had not realized that rhetoric is every bit as important as reason. Through his own example in *Leviathan*, he has shown how reason and eloquence can be combined for the benefit of the people. Indeed, he gives a specific example of a friend of his, Sidney Godolphin, who combines these traits perfectly, and therefore could provide a great model for leadership using Hobbes's science. Hobbes differentiates moral science from natural science precisely on this need for eloquence to advance moral truths: 'So also reason, and eloquence, though not perhaps in the natural sciences, yet, in the moral, may stand very well together. For wheresoever there is place for adorning and preferring of error, there is much more place for adorning and preferring of truth' (504).

One place where Hobbes attempts to shore up his previous reasoning is in the area of military service (see chapter 15 of *Leviathan*). Hobbes makes a more forthright statement here that a man is obliged to protect the sovereign authority in war, because that authority also protects him. You may recall the problem we discussed earlier about the seeming contradiction between the right to self-preservation and the obligation to military service. Here Hobbes strengthens the idea that a soldier is obliged to fight because of his agreement to serve. But Hobbes also repeats his argument that if the same man feels he is no longer protected in the field (for instance, if the forces are scattered and he cannot count on help from his fellow soldiers), then he is free to seek protection from another power. No doubt Hobbes was aware of criticisms that he was encouraging cowardice and desertion. He was trying to counter these criticisms, but with how much success it is up to the reader to decide.

Hobbes also tries here to dissuade leaders from basing their authority on anything other than their power. He points out that, when sovereigns point to the history of their family and some ancient right, they create more problems than they solve. Because 'there is scarce a commonwealth in the world, whose beginnings can in conscience be justified', pointing back to those beginnings (which almost always involve unjust force and usurpation) simply gives people fodder for criticism and rebellion. Hobbes is calling upon sovereigns to leave aside these romantic justifications for their power and simply tell the truth – that they have legitimate power because they provide peace and protection to their people.

Towards the end, Hobbes acknowledges that in his section on the Christian Commonwealth he has expounded some 'new doctrines', which some may criticize as unauthorized. But Hobbes appeals to the extraordinary times in which he lived (as we saw him do in the final chapter) to justify his boldness. In an allusion to Christ's own words that his teaching was 'new wine' which should not be put into old skins, Hobbes calls his own teaching 'new wine, to put into new casks, that both may be preserved together' (509). In other words, the times were so chaotic, and there had been so many new and challenging interpretations of Christian duty, that the door was open to Hobbes's interpretation also. Perhaps it could be put into minds ready to receive a new doctrine that could save their lives, if not their souls!

Hobbes also defends himself against the charge that he has neglected the authority of 'ancient poets, orators, and philosophers' (510) and has not quoted them to support his views. Hobbes's reasons for not doing so we can already guess. But here, he says that 'the matters in question are not of *fact*, but of *right*, wherein there is no place for *witnesses*' (510). That is, they are not about previous events, or even historical proof, let alone the authority of previous thinkers. Hobbes's arguments stem from nature and natural right, which is a way of thinking unbound by time and authority. That is why within this type of argument there is 'no place for *witnesses*', no need for the confirmation of history or other authors. Either Hobbes's reasons, which derive from his theory of nature, are sound or they are not. Reason can judge the question unaided by ancient or modern poets, orators or philosophers. Hobbes wryly suggests that these authorities probably knew less than Hobbes knows: 'For if we will reverence the age, the present is the oldest. If the antiquity of the writer, I am not sure, that generally they to whom such honour is given, were more ancient when they wrote, than I am that am writing. But if it be well considered, the praise of ancient authors, proceeds not from the reverence of the dead, but from the competition, and mutual envy of the living' (510).

In addition to displaying that marvellous humour we have come to expect in Hobbes's writing, this statement wonderfully displays the modern mentality regarding the past. Whereas traditional societies reverence the past as superior to their own, full of wisdom which must be transmitted and cannot be supplemented, the modern thinker believes that knowledge is cumulative, that the ancients were relatively ignorant, and that the present age is wise by comparison.

Hobbes ends by urging again that his doctrine promotes peace and that it ought to be taught in universities and preached in churches. He believes that if the leaders and the common people understand the basis of government, and thus the 'mutual relationship between protection and obedience' (511), they can become active partners in the strengthening of their commonwealth instead of hapless dupes of ambitious clergy and other sophists. Whereas in times past it might have seemed an asset, Hobbes clearly believes that an ignorant populace is now a liability. Education, of course, should not encourage critical thinking concerning government authority, but it should encourage true understanding of the reason for that authority. From now on, the people must help uphold the stability of the state. This new relationship between the people and their government, however, could not be held within the boundaries which Hobbes constructed. As you will see if you go on to read Locke, it fairly quickly changed into an argument against absolutism.

## Question

1. In the 'Review and Conclusion', can you see what Hobbes thinks is his unique role in bringing necessary changes to the political order?

# CHAPTER 4

# RECEPTION AND INFLUENCE

## HOBBES'S CONTEMPORARIES

It would probably be an understatement to say that many prominent people disliked Hobbes during his lifetime. Hobbes was reviled in articles, speeches, from the pulpit, and even in parliament. If Hobbes was disliked, it was because of what he wrote. 'There were three main charges: that he was an atheist (or, at least, guilty of gross heresies), that his political theory glorified despotism, and that he overturned traditional morality. The third charge connected the first and the second: he was accused of deriving morality not from God or reason but from the will of the sovereign' (Malcolm 2004).

In other words, critics noticed that Hobbes's political philosophy took aim at dearly held religious and moral beliefs, questioned them, re-examined them, and deconstructed them. In practical terms, he did derive morality from the will of the sovereign rather than God or reason, and this got him into a lot of trouble.

Samuel Mintz has provided an excellent record and analysis of seventeenth-century reactions to Hobbes in *The Hunting of Leviathan* (1962). Mintz divides Hobbes's contemporary enemies into three groups: 'the clergy and sectaries of all persuasions, the university teachers, and the lawyers' (46). As we have seen, Hobbes attacked all three of these groups as subversive, so it should not come as a shock that they saw Hobbes the same way. But Mintz convincingly argues that all of Hobbes's critics, while certainly attempting to protect their privileged positions, were also genuinely shocked at what they thought was Hobbes's dangerous blasphemy and atheism. More than anything else, it was Hobbes's radical materialism that outraged them, particularly his insistence that spirits and even God must be material to have any existence at all. This materialism, coupled with his deconstruction of prophecy, biblical authorship, and Heaven and Hell, were enough to make his critics not only angry but also afraid of Hobbes and what he stood for. Books and articles were written from almost every perspective – dissenting Protestant, Anglican, Catholic – accusing Hobbes of the most dastardly subversion of all that was good and holy. Hobbes's name became 'a by-word for infidelity' (Mintz 1962: 55).

After the Restoration of Charles II, a bill was introduced into the House of Commons which banned 'blasphemous books, among which *Leviathan* was listed . . . In 1666, with some people believing that the London plague of 1665 and the Great Fire of 1666 were God's punishment for Hobbes's presence in the city' (Reilly 2001), a bill was introduced in parliament to investigate Hobbes for atheism. But, with the help of friends in the court of the restored Charles II, the bill disappeared in a committee (Martinich 2003). Charles, however, forbade Hobbes to publish any political or religious books, and those already in print were burned. This was not the first time Hobbes's books had been burned, nor would it be the last.

Hobbes became notorious not only for his ideas but also his squabbles with members of the Royal Society for the Promotion of Natural Knowledge, a prestigious scholarly body to which Hobbes was never admitted, because its members were concerned for its reputation. But Hobbes was not universally disliked. He had many friends and admirers. John Aubrey, a friend of Hobbes, whose *Brief Lives* chronicles many of the greatest men of the times, wrote a biography of Hobbes that is glowing, almost to the point of hero-worship (Aubrey 1950: 147–59). Quentin Skinner argues convincingly that many scholars have overplayed Hobbes's unpopularity. While he was often the target of criticism in England, Skinner argues that his reputation was better in Europe. He was welcomed into intellectual circles in France, where he found sanctuary during the English Civil War, and where he met some of the greatest minds of his age (Skinner 1966: 288). 'The failure to acknowledge this element of popularity has tended to give a misleading impression of the intentions of Hobbes's contemporary critics. They have been treated as attacking a single source of heterodox opinion. It can be shown, however, that they concentrated on Hobbes not because he was seen as the "singlehanded" opponent of tradition, but rather because he was seen to give the ablest and most influential presentation to a point of view which was itself gaining increasingly in fashionable acceptance and in ideological importance' (Skinner 1966: 295).

Also, we must remember that while Hobbes was being roundly attacked in influential circles, *Leviathan* and other works by him continued to grow in popularity, even when they were officially banned or condemned. *Leviathan* was published multiple times, sometimes secretly, and its desirability increased as the condemnations continued (Mintz 1962: 61). Perhaps this should have served as a lesson to Hobbes's critics. Sometimes the more a work is condemned, the more popular it becomes! Skinner argues that, acknowledged or not, Hobbes's work was of great influence on many of his contemporaries. They borrowed from his methods and ideas, but because of Hobbes's shaky reputation, did not give him proper attribution (Skinner 1966: 305).

Despite the image of Hobbes as the evil atheist, Hobbes the man was capable of great personal kindness and even piety. When he died, he left a considerable portion of his estate to a Miss Elizabeth Alaby, and also requested that she be married to his executor's son, Jack Wheldon, 'provided they liked one another, and that he was not a Spendthrift' (Reilly 2001). The attention paid to Alaby in his will spurred some speculation that she was Hobbes's illegitimate daughter, but there is no evidence for this. Instead, she appears to have been an orphan, abandoned at about five years old, whom Hobbes decided to rescue. His will also left money to the poor and to the minister of the parish in which he was buried. It is safe to say that Hobbes was not an evil man and indeed acted as an upright and good man in his personal life. His critics, however, thought that his ideas were subversive of religion and morality and had therefore to be vigorously opposed.

## INFLUENCE ON POLITICAL PHILOSOPHY

Another way to measure Hobbes's influence is to trace the advancement of his ideas in the subsequent history of political philosophy. One can see Hobbesian ideas in the writings of philosopher of international law Samuel Puffendorf, in Hobbes's contemporary Spinoza, and in utilitarian thought (Watkins 1957: 355). One can also see his influence on twentieth-century social contract thinkers such as John Rawls. But we can see Hobbes's influence most clearly in the development of the classical liberal philosophy of John Locke, which provided the intellectual backdrop for England's Glorious Revolution of 1688.

Hobbes's influence can be seen in Locke's views on religion. This is surprising, given their seemingly very different conclusions on the issue. But as Robert Kraynak (1990) points out, Hobbes and Locke are both Enlightenment thinkers (Hobbes as a precursor to Enlightenment thought) and are much more similar on religion and politics than is usually assumed. Indeed, Kraynak locates the very origins of the Enlightenment in Hobbes, whose thought is characterized by the rejection of orthodoxy and authority. For Hobbes, this rejection leads inevitably to absolutism – moral truth is subjective and causes conflict, hence the need for the public imposition of truth. But Kraynak demonstrates that the same problem of religious conflict that led Hobbes to argue for absolutism eventually led Locke to favour toleration, and that Locke followed much of Hobbes's reasoning.

Locke, in his early *Two Tracts on Government*, actually defended absolutism much as Hobbes did. Locke lamented the devastation caused by religious zealotry and sectarianism and initially attempted, like Hobbes, to argue for the absolute right of the sovereign to control all outward signs of religion. In reaction to what he saw as the divisiveness and intolerance of Catholics, Anglicans and Dissenters, he claimed like Hobbes that the mode of public worship should be deemed 'indifferent' (irrelevant) as long as it honoured God. He agreed with Hobbes that such public worship did not impinge upon inward beliefs, so it could be done without infringing upon the worshippers' conscience (Kraynak 1980). Thus, early in his career, Locke set up the same dichotomy as Hobbes between public worship and private belief. But 'Locke soon realized that his effort to gain admission of indifferency and acceptance of uniformity would be difficult or impossible' (Kraynak 1980: 59).

In other words, Locke came to realize that people could not be persuaded to accept his claim that how people worshipped did not matter. Locke realized that 'secular absolutism depends on a kind of enlightened cynicism. Before people will accept arbitrary imposition, they must be liberated from belief' (Kraynak 1980: 60). But few people were capable of such enlightened cynicism, so Locke turned to toleration as a superior way of managing the same sectarian conflict that so bedevilled Hobbes.

The most obvious area of influence between Hobbes and Locke is located in the ideas surrounding the state of nature, the laws of nature, and the social contract.[1] As we have seen, Hobbes starts the development of his philosophy with assumptions about human nature, and then asks how human beings such as he describes would behave under conditions of anarchy. For Hobbes, people would know what it takes to bring peace (the laws of nature), but they would not be able to pursue peace because they would not feel secure. Their first right of nature was self-preservation, and in anarchy that right trumped all other rights and duties. Justice and injustice, right and wrong, could have no meaning in the state of nature. Hobbes then showed how the only way out, the only way to guarantee self-preservation, was to establish a social contract, an agreement among each individual with every other individual, to surrender their independent powers to an all-powerful sovereign. Only then, in Hobbes's view, could people achieve peace and begin to prosper and advance.

Locke took Hobbes's framework, including the state of nature, natural laws, and the social contract, but he changed some of the assumptions, in particular those about human nature. While people were far from morally perfect, to Locke it seemed wrong to say that human beings were the anti-social, violent, completely untrustworthy beings Hobbes made them out to be. For Locke, human beings wanted to join together to form societies and did so naturally and informally. Also, people knew the laws of nature and could follow them most of the time, even in the state of nature. So, 'people may make promises and contracts with one another, transfer rights and undertake obligations, without leaving the state of nature' (Simmons 1989: 452). But without government, their adherence to the laws of nature would always be imperfect. For instance, if some of their property was stolen, instead of simply taking it back to establish justice, or taking something proportional from their enemy, people were likely to turn to excessive measures. According to Locke, people find it hard to be impartial or objective in matters that personally concern them. So, in the state of nature, crime was more likely to happen and excessive punishment – and therefore ongoing feuds – were the likely result. This situation, while livable, was not very pleasant and did not allow people to build up much in the way of personal property, because their property could not extend past that which they could defend by themselves.

So, for Locke, people established a government through a social contract in order to protect their lives, but also (and unlike Hobbes) their property and their liberty. Since Locke's state of nature was livable and relatively free and had a modicum of justice, Locke reasoned that people would choose to live in that state rather than choose an absolute government. If they did decide to make a government, it would have to do more for people than simply protect their lives. Locke would ask Hobbes and other absolutists why people in the state of nature would give up their independence and enslave themselves to a tyrannical government. Would it not be better to remain in nature? So Locke's theory veers off in a different direction than Hobbes's and ends up going exactly where Hobbes never wants to go: establishing a natural right to revolution.

In Locke's view, going back to the state of nature may be the best option if faced with tyranny. Locke's conclusions may just be where social contract thinking inevitably ends up, despite Hobbes's best efforts to make it move in the opposite direction.

## MODERN INTERPRETATIONS OF HOBBES

Much of the modern scholarship on Hobbes asks the same question his contemporaries had – what did Hobbes really think about religion and how integral was Hobbes's interpretation of Christian theology to the rest of his political philosophy? Leo Strauss saw Hobbes's political philosophy as capable of standing on its own, without his theological teachings, and questioned whether Hobbes's statements on religion were sincere or merely useful. He said that Hobbes's purpose was first to 'make use of the authority of the Scriptures for his own theory, and next and particularly in order to shake the authority of the Scriptures themselves' (Strauss 1984: 71). From this perspective, Hobbes could very well have been an atheist, a precursor of the Enlightenment criticism of religion.

Paul Cooke is another scholar who disputes the current tendency to take Hobbes's Christianity seriously as a guiding impulse in his works. Cooke's approach is to examine what Hobbes says about religion in his philosophic works and then ask if any believing Christian could hold such views. Much like Strauss, Cooke concludes that Hobbes was rejecting any common notion of Christian beliefs and subordinating consideration of those beliefs to his earthly political programme (Cooke 1996).

On the other hand, A.P. Martinich (1992) finds in Hobbes someone who is making a sincere attempt to show how Christian beliefs can support his political theory, even if his biblical interpretations and theology are unorthodox. Martinich thinks that while 'the consensus of scholarly opinion now counts him a tepid theist' (1992: 1), Hobbes was actually a sincere, orthodox Calvinist who was attempting to preserve the relevance and validity of the scripture in light of the new science of Copernicus and Galileo. From this perspective, Hobbes wanted to show that religion need not be a politically destabilizing force (Martinich 1992). Joshua Mitchell also claims that Hobbes is very much within the Protestant orb, attempting to answer the question of the relationship between Moses and Christ, or the Old and the New Testament. But whereas Protestants saw the New Testament superseding the Old, Hobbes saw it as a relationship of renewal and fulfilment. Mitchell argues that for Hobbes, 'Christ's covenant [is] fulfilled in Hobbes's England' (Mitchell 1993: 93). However, other scholars, like Hiram Caton, question 'If the theology of Hobbes was Calvinist and sincere, where are the Calvinist clergymen who so witness? What Puritan ever said that Christianity reduces to one dogma [that Jesus is Christ]?' (Caton 1994: 112).

Another way of sorting through the question of Hobbes's relationship to Christianity is to see the bigger picture of Hobbes as a political philosopher within the Western Judeo-Christian tradition. From this vantage point, Hobbes's thought still reflects that tradition even as it offers up a profound critique. For example, Joshua Mitchell sees Hobbes's entire political theory, with its message of 'equality of all under the one', as secularized Christian theology and thus ultimately as a product of the Christian world-view (1993: 91). Likewise, Howard Warrender claims that 'Hobbes is essentially a natural law philosopher', and thus has taken a system Christian in origin, secularized it, and innovated on it (1993: 938).

Another issue that scholars wrangle over is how to interpret Hobbes in the first place. Should we primarily look at the internal logic of his works and employ the method of careful reading, or should we look for an explanation in the historical and cultural context in which he lived? While all scholars use both methods of interpretation when researching Hobbes as well as any other thinker, this is a matter of emphasis, and involves some fairly significant disagreements. Leo Strauss's (1984) method, for instance, was primarily the former. He believed that interpreting a thinker as a product of his times led to 'historicism', the reduction of the thinker's ideas to historical artefacts without lasting meaning. But Strauss can see within Hobbes's theory influences from ideas across the centuries and from many different sources, as well as a claim to voicing universal truths about human nature and politics which need to be taken seriously in order to be fully understood.

Warrender agrees: 'The classic texts in political philosophy are more than tracts for the times. However much they are involved with and illuminate the author's immediate context, they continue to be studied for what insight they offer in new and changing situations. To consign them to their contemporary milieu, with whatever honours, is to bury them. Hobbes more than most has preserved his relevance and justified his own claim not to be placed on a limited historical stage, but to be regarded as writing for all time' (1979: 939).

On the other side of this debate stands Quentin Skinner and the Cambridge school from which he comes. Skinner has strongly criticized the Straussian approach (Wiener 1974: 251). Skinner's method involves studying the use of language surrounding the author and his times and the debates and issues at the fore of the author's consciousness. Skinner would argue that without this type of study, we cannot really know the author's intentions. Using this method, Skinner argues that Hobbes's *Leviathan* can be seen as providing arguments for those who wished to submit to the authority of the revolutionary Puritan government and thus Hobbes was actually a partisan of 'Engagement' with that government and not the rabid advocate of absolutism many commentators have seen. Under Skinner's pen, Hobbes becomes a humanist, an advocate of republican government, and a believer in the supreme power of rhetoric (Skinner 1996).

However, a recent critic of Skinner has taken his method to task for being selective and over-reaching. While advocates of engagement used some of Hobbes's arguments for their own purposes, 'it is not even clear that Hobbes realized his argument could be used as the Engagers used it'. An aspect of the historical context Skinner leaves out makes his conclusions about Hobbes unlikely at best – 'Hobbes was a committed royalist and had life-long ties to the monarchy – ties that continued, it should be stressed, after the Restoration' (Goodhart 2000: 547). Goodheart ends his critique by suggesting a hidden motive for Skinner's re-writing (in his view) of Hobbes's history – 'to undermine the very foundations of much of contemporary liberal thought' in favour of the Cambridge school's preferred republicanism (2000: 560).

Given the endless ways in which the historical approach can be dissected and critiqued, one can see why many scholars have come to doubt whether it can ever provide certainty about an author's intentions. However, Mintz's work, *The Hunting of Leviathan*, referenced above, is a good example of how learning more about the people around Hobbes, both critics and admirers, can help us understand what he was doing and his impact during his lifetime. For instance, as Mintz (1962) points out, we can rule out the argument that Hobbes's Christian theology was simply a ruse to keep him from being accused of atheism, because he was indeed frequently accused of atheism and even provoked parliament to contemplate charges of atheism. If he was trying to avoid such charges, he would have changed his strategy. There are certainly insights that one can draw only by taking into account the author's context.

Clearly, different scholars focus on different aspects of Hobbes, often with surprisingly diverse results. We have seen Quentin Skinner (1996) assert that Hobbes was a republican philosopher. C. B. Macpherson, on the other hand, saw in Hobbes's philosophy a defence of bourgeois 'possessive individualism' (Macpherson 1962). Michael Oakeshott traced the overriding theme of rationalism in Hobbes's thought (Oakeshott 1975), while Strauss and Warrender saw Hobbes as a modern moral philosopher (Spragens 1978: 652).

Spragens may speak for most readers when he complains that by narrowing their focus to particular issues of their own, each of these authors 'unnecessarily obscures both the genuine elements of unity in Hobbes' thought and the impact of Hobbes' profound aspirations to be "scientific"' (Spragens 1978: 652). Nevertheless, each perspective, while sometimes more bent on making the author's point than explaining Hobbes's point, contributes to our knowledge of Hobbes's theory, his intentions, and his impact. If we read widely enough in this literature, we can come to a rounded and more mature view of Hobbes's philosophy.

# CHAPTER 5

# GUIDE TO FURTHER READING

## EDITIONS OF *LEVIATHAN*

There are numerous editions of *Leviathan* in print today. At least ten editions are readily available in Internet bookstores. There are no English 'translations' of *Leviathan*, since it was originally written in English. (There is, however, Hobbes's own translation of *Leviathan into* Latin, published in 1668, when Hobbes was 80.) Nor can we find 'modern' versions of *Leviathan* in which the English has been updated to reflect modern usage and vernacular. Many editions contain Hobbes's original antiquated English with its erratic spelling, but readers can also find editions in which the spelling and punctuation has been standardized. While Hobbes's writing style takes some getting used to, scholars agree that it is always best to approach a text in the original if at all possible. After all, any translation, even to modernized English, cannot help but change the meaning, sometimes subtly, sometimes quite radically, depending on the translator. This book has employed the Oakeshott edition of *Leviathan*, listed below, which standardizes Hobbes's spelling. Standardizing spelling does not interfere with meaning and it is an acceptable accommodation for more comfortable reading.

Below is a short list of those editions of *Leviathan* in print which the reader might find particularly useful, either for the editors' introductions, scholarly notes, or other editorial features:

1. Thomas Hobbes, *Leviathan*, edited by Michael Oakeshott, New York: Simon & Schuster, Touchstone edition, 1997. The virtue of this edition is Oakeshott's editing, which standardizes

Hobbes's spelling but does not change his sentence structure. There is an introduction by Richard S. Peters.

2. Thomas Hobbes, *Leviathan: With Selected Variants from the Latin Edition of 1668*, edited by Edwin Curley, Indianapolis: Hackett Publishing Company, 1994. This edition also standardizes the spelling and provides content from Hobbes's Latin version of *Leviathan*, showing how the content sometimes differed between the English and Latin versions. Curley provides excellent biographical information and a bibliography.

3. Thomas Hobbes, *Hobbes: Leviathan: Revised student edition (Cambridge Texts in the History of Political Thought)*, Cambridge: Cambridge University Press, 1996. This edition, part of a series edited by Quentin Skinner, keeps the original English. Richard Tuck provides the introduction and there is a useful chronology, a guide to further reading, and biographies of important figures featured in *Leviathan*.

4. Thomas Hobbes, *Leviathan,* edited by Karl Schumann and G.A.J. Rogers, Thoemmes Continuum, 2003 (new edition available in 2006). This two-volume set is a good choice for the scholar, containing detailed information on the different versions of *Leviathan*, including the Latin version. It deals extensively with *Leviathan*'s publication history and the various changes Hobbes made to the text along the way.

5. Thomas Hobbes, *Leviathan*, edited by C.B. Macpherson, New York: Penguin Classics, 1985. This edition contains an introduction by Macpherson, who famously analysed Hobbes as an advocate of 'possessive individualism'. This *Leviathan* retains Hobbes's original English.

Hobbes's English corpus can be found in most university libraries under the title *The English Works of Thomas Hobbes*. Students and other scholars might be interested in the Past Masters electronic version of Hobbes's *English Works* which, of course, includes *Leviathan*, and makes the entire *English Works* readily available on computer. The Past Masters software allows the researcher to quickly trace words and phrases throughout Hobbes's works, locate Hobbes's thoughts on particular ideas, and quote and cite Hobbes. Some libraries have Past Masters software available in their reference sections, or it is available for sale at: http://www.nlx.com/pstm/

## Secondary Material

There is one academic journal entirely devoted to Hobbes: *Hobbes Studies*, published once a year. There have been so many books and articles written on all aspects of Hobbes and his political theory that it is impossible to list them all. What follows is a bibliography of works which students and other scholars might find particularly useful in doing research on Hobbes, broken down by topic.

### HISTORICAL BACKGROUND

Aubrey, John, *Brief Lives*, ed. Oliver Lawson Dick, London: Secker and Warburg, 1950.
Fletcher, Anthony, *The Outbreak of the English Civil War*, London: Edward Arnold, Ltd, 1981.
Kraynak, Robert P., *History and Modernity in the Thought of Thomas Hobbes*, Ithaca: Cornell University Press, 1990.
Martinich, A.P., *Hobbes: A Biography*, Cambridge: Cambridge University Press, 1999.
Mintz, Samuel, *The Hunting of* Leviathan: *Seventeenth Century Reactions to the Materialism and Moral Philosophy of Thomas Hobbes*, Cambridge: Cambridge University Press, 1962.
Shapiro, Barbara J., 'The Universities and Science in Seventeenth Century England,' *The Journal of British Studies* 10.2 (May 1971): 72.
Tuck, Richard (ed.), *Philosophy and Government 1571–1651*, Cambridge: Cambridge University Press, 1993.
Woolrych, Austin, *Britain in Revolution: 1625–1660*, Oxford: Oxford University Press, 2002.
Zagorin, Peter, 'Hobbes's Early Philosophical Development', *Journal of the History of Ideas* 54.3 (July 1993): 505–18.

### HOBBES'S POLITICAL THEORY

Baumbold, Deborah, *Hobbes' Political Theory*, Cambridge: Cambridge University Press, 1988.
Dietz, Mary G. (ed.), *Thomas Hobbes and Political Theory*, Lawrence, KS: University Press of Kansas, 1990.
Gauthier, David, *The Logic of* Leviathan: *The Moral & Political Theory of Thomas Hobbes*, London: Oxford University Press, 2001.
Green, Arnold W., *Hobbes and Human Nature*, New Brunswick: Transaction Publishers, 1993.
Hampton, Jean, *Hobbes and the Social Contract Tradition*, Cambridge: Cambridge University Press, 1988.

### INTERNATIONAL RELATIONS

Bagby, Laurie M. Johnson, ' "Mathematici" v. "Dogmatici": Understanding the Realist Project Through Hobbes', *Interpretation: A Journal of Political Philosophy* 29.1 (Spring 2002): 281–97.

Brown, Clifford W., Jr., 'Thucydides, Hobbes, and the Derivation of Anarchy', *History of Political Thought* 8.1 (Spring 1987): 33–62.

Boucher, David, 'Inter-Community & International Relations in the Political Philosophy of Hobbes', *Polity* 23.2 (Winter 1990): 207–32.

Bull, Hedley, 'Hobbes and the International Anarchy', *Social Research* 48.4 (Winter 1981): 717–38.

Klosko, George, and Daryl Rice, 'Thucydides and Hobbes's State of Nature', *History of Political Thought* 7.3 (Winter 1985): 405–9.

Kraynak, Robert P., 'Hobbes on Barbarism and Civilization,' *The Journal of Politics* 45.1 (February 1983): 86–109.

Williams, Michael C., 'Hobbes and International Relations: A Reconsideration', *International Organization* 50.2 (Spring 1996): 213–36.

## INTERPRETATIONS OF HOBBES'S THEORY

Cantalupo, Charles, *A Literary* Leviathan: *Thomas Hobbes's Masterpiece of Language*, London and Toronto: Associated University Presses, 1991.

Caton, Hiram, 'Is Leviathan a Unicorn? Varieties of Hobbes Interpretations,' *The Review of Politics* 56.1 (Winter 1994): 101–25.

Johnston, David, *The Rhetoric of* Leviathan: *Thomas Hobbes and the Politics of Cultural Transformation*, Princeton: Princeton University Press, 1986.

Macpherson, C.B., *The Political Theory of Possessive Individualism: Hobbes to Locke*, Oxford: Clarendon Press, 1964.

Martinich, A.P., 'Interpretation and Hobbes's Political Philosophy,' *Pacific Philosophical Quarterly* 82.3 (September 2001): 309–31.

Oakeshott, Michael, *Hobbes on Civil Association*, Berkeley: University of California Press, 1975.

— *Rationalism in Politics and Other Essays*, Indianapolis: LibertyPress, 1991.

Reik, Miriam M., *The Golden Lands of Thomas Hobbes*, Detroit: Wayne State University Press, 1977.

Rogow, Arnold A., *Thomas Hobbes: Radical in the Service of Reaction*, New York: W.W. Norton, 1986.

Skinner, Quentin, *Reason and Rhetoric in the Philosophy of* Leviathan, Cambridge: Cambridge University Press, 1996.

Slomp, Gabriella, *Thomas Hobbes and the Political Philosophy of Glory*, New York: Saint Martin's Press, 2000.

Spragens, Thomas A. Jr., *The Politics of Motion: The World of Thomas Hobbes*, Lexington: The University of Kentucky Press, 1973.

Strauss, Leo, *Natural Right and History*, Chicago: University of Chicago Press, 1968.

Strauss, Leo, *The Political Philosophy of Hobbes: Its Basis and Its Genesis*, trans. Elsa M. Sinclair, Chicago: University of Chicago Press, 1984.

Sullivan, Vickie B, *Machiavelli, Hobbes, and the Formation of a Liberal Republicanism in England*, Cambridge: Cambridge University Press, 2004.

Tarlton, C., 'The Despotical Doctrine of Hobbes, Part I: the Liberalization of *Leviathan*', *History of Political Thought* 22.4 (2001): 587–619.

Tarlton, C., 'The Despotical Doctrine of Hobbes, Part II: Aspects of the Textual Substructure of Tyranny in Leviathan,' *History of Political Thought* 23.1 (2002): 62–90.


## REFERENCE

Hinnant, Charles H., *Thomas Hobbes: A Reference Guide*, Boston: G.K. Hall, 1980.
Martinich, A.P., *A Hobbes Dictionary*, London: Blackwell, 1995.
Sacksteder, William, *Hobbes Studies (1879–1979): A Bibliography*, Bowling Green: Philosophy Documentation Center, Bowling Green State University, 1982.
Sorell, Tom (ed.), *The Cambridge Companion to Hobbes*, Cambridge: Cambridge University Press, 1996.


## RELIGION

Cooke, Paul., *Hobbes and Christianity: Reassessing the Bible in* Leviathan, New York: Rowan and Littlefield Publishers, Inc., 1996.
Martinich, A.P., *The Two Gods of* Leviathan: *Thomas Hobbes on Religion and Politics*, New York: Cambridge University Press, 1992.
Milner, Benjamin, 'Hobbes: On Religion,' *Political Theory* 16.3 (August 1988): 400–25.
Mitchell, Joshua, 'Hobbes and the Equality of All under the One', *Political Theory* 21.3 (February 1993): 78–100.
— 'Luther and Hobbes on the Question: Who Was Moses? Who Was Christ?', *The Journal of Politics* 53.3 (August 1991): 676–700.
Shulman, George, 'Hobbes, Puritans and Promethean Politics', *Political Theory* 16.3 (August 1988): 426–43.


## WOMEN AND FAMILY

Carver, Terrell, 'Public Man and the Critique of Masculinities', *Political Theory* 24.4 (November 1996): 673–86.
Chapman, Richard Allen. '*Leviathan* Writ Small: Thomas Hobbes on the Family', *The American Political Science Review* 69.1 (March 1975): 76–90.
Pateman, Carole, 'God Hath Ordained to Man a Helper: Hobbes, Patriarchy and Conjugal Right', *British Journal of Political Science* 19.4 (October 1989): 445–63.
Pateman, Carole, Hirschmann, Nancy J., and Powell Jr., Bingham, 'Political Obligation, Freedom and Feminism', *The American Political Science Review* 86.1 (March 1992): 179–88.
Schochet, Gordon J., 'Thomas Hobbes on the Family and the State of Nature', *Political Science Quarterly* 82.3. (September 1967): 427–45.
Wright, H. 'Going Against the Grain: Hobbes's Case for Original Maternal Dominion', *Journal of Women's History* 14.1 (Spring 2002): 123–50.

# NOTES

## 1. CONTEXT AND INTRODUCTION

1 See Malcolm 2004.
2 Ibid.
3 See Martinich (1999), chs 6 and 7, for a thorough account of this time in exile.
4 On this theme see Shulman 1988: 426–43.
5 Joshua Mitchell argues that Hobbes's political philosophy is derived from these very Protestant ideas, especially equality of all before God, and secularized, to create a modern political philosophy for a changing world. See Mitchell 1993, especially 86–8.

## 2. OVERVIEW OF THEMES

1 Any quotations of the Bible that are mine come from the Douay–Rheims Version.
2 For insightful comments on this image, see Strong 1993 and Springborg 1995.

## 3. READING THE TEXT

1 See Peters' treatment (1967) of the issue of accurate speech in chapter 5, 'Speech', 112–28.
2 Shulman 1988 develops this idea of Promethean politics in his article.
3 For an old but good discussion of the social contract and the idea that obligation in Hobbes rests exclusively on self-interest, see Nagel 1959.
4 For a great discussion of this section, see Hoekstra 1997.
5 For a good discussion of representation and authorization under the covenant, see Baumgold 1988, chapter 3.
6 Because of Hobbes's clear preference for monarchy, subsequent references to 'the sovereign', in this book can be assumed to be references to the sovereign monarch.

7  For more information on this topic, see Schrock 1991, who argues that none of Hobbes's attempts to establish the government's right to punish work, in light of the subjects' right to resist.

8  Latin translation mine.

9  Hobbes talks more about the proper relationship among God, the sovereign, his subordinate officials and the people in Part III of *Leviathan*, 'Of a Christian Commonwealth'.

10  For a lengthier discussion of this aspect of Hobbes's thought see Seaman 1990.

11  See Martinich's excellent treatment (1992) of the Kingdom of God and sovereign-making covenants in chapter 6.

12  For an excellent account of Hobbes's reason and purpose in writing the second half of *Leviathan* see Cooke.

13  For more on these differences among scholars, see the section on Hobbes's reception and influence.

14  The captivity referred to here is the Babylonian Captivity of the Jews, which happened around the fifth century BC, in which many of the Jews were taken from Jerusalem into slavery in Babylon and others were dispersed.

15  For an excellent discussion of Hobbes's analysis of the kingdom of God, see Milner 1988.

16  Another excellent discussion of the kingdom of God theme is in Johnston 1986. He examines the rhetorical dimension of this theme. 'Hobbes's refounding of Christianity was an attempt', he writes, 'to transform men and women into the rational and predictable beings they would have to be before his vision of political society could ever be realized' (184).

17  For a good look at Hobbes's attitude towards the Puritan Protestants, see Shulman 1988.

18  For a great treatment of this part of *Leviathan,* see Martinich 1992, especially chapter 11, 'Scripture'.

19  Protestants agreed with Hobbes, against the Catholic church's view, that the age of miracles had ended, Milner writes, 'But the reformers distinguish those public miracles of the Holy Spirit from his invisible work in the hearts of men, which they do not hesitate to call supernatural' (Milner 1988: 412).

20  Another thinker Hobbes cites is Theodore Beza (by his last name only), the successor of John Calvin in Geneva, to whom he also attributes the teaching that the kingdom of God began at the time of the resurrection and exists in the world today.

21  See Strong 1993: 137–8. Hobbes was on firm ground with Protestants of all types with his denial of Purgatory.

22  Strong 1993 locates Hobbes as closer to Luther than Calvin on this issue, but as going further than Luther, who thought souls slept and did not die (138).

23  On this point see Springborg 1994, especially 555.

24  Aristotle disagreed with Plato about the existence of the forms, reasoning that ideals must be derived from things as they actually exist in the

world. Nonetheless, Hobbes could still apply his criticism to Aristotle's thought because Aristotle still formulated ideals that were treated in practice as separate from any given instance, and also developed in his own way the idea of the human soul.

## 4. RECEPTION AND INFLUENCE

1 For a good discussion of Hobbes's influence on Locke see Coby 1987.

# BIBLIOGRAPHY

What follows is a bibliography of works cited in this book.

Aubrey, John, *Brief Lives*, ed. Oliver Lawson Dick, London: Secker and Warburg, 1950.

Baumbold, Deborah, *Hobbes' Political Theory*, Cambridge: Cambridge University Press, 1988.

Caton, Hiram, 'Is Leviathan a Unicorn? Varieties of Hobbes Interpretations', *The Review of Politics* 56.1 (Winter 1994): 101–25.

Coby, Patrick, 'The Law of Nature in Locke's *Second Treatise*: Is Locke a Hobbesian?', *The Review of Politics* 49.1 (Winter 1987): 3–28.

Cooke, Paul, *Hobbes and Christianity: Reassessing the Bible in* Leviathan, New York: Rowan and Littlefield Publishers, Inc., 1996.

Goodhart, Michael, 'Theory in Practice: Quentin Skinner's Hobbes, Reconsidered', *The Review of Politics* 6.3 (Summer 2000): 531–61.

Grant, Hardy, 'Geometry and Politics: Mathematics in the Thought of Thomas Hobbes,' *Mathematics Magazine* 63.3 (June 1990): 147–54.

Hobbes, Thomas, *Behemoth or the Long Parliament*, Chicago: University of Chicago Press, 1990.

— *Hobbes's Thucydides*, ed. Richard Schlatter, New Brunswick: Rutgers University Press, 1975.

— *Leviathan*, New York: Macmillan Publishing Company, 1962.

Hoekstra, Kinch, 'Hobbes and the Foole', *Political Theory* 25.5 (October 1997): 620–54.

Johnston, David, *The Rhetoric of* Leviathan: *Thomas Hobbes and the Politics of Cultural Transformation*, Princeton: Princeton University Press, 1986.

Kraynak, Robert P., *History and Modernity in the Thought of Thomas Hobbes*, Ithaca: Cornell University Press, 1990.

Kraynak, Robert P., 'John Locke: From Absolutism to Toleration', *The American Political Science Review* 74.1 (March 1980): 53–69.

Locke, John, 'Letter Concerning Toleration', The Hague: M. Nijhoff, 1963.

— *Two Tracts on Government*, ed., Philip Abrams, London: Cambridge University Press, 1967.

—— *Two Treatises of Government*, London: Cambridge University Press, 1960.

Macpherson, C.B., *The Political Theory of Possessive Individualism: Hobbes to Locke*, Oxford: Clarendon Press, 1962.

Malcolm, Noel, 'Hobbes, Thomas (1588–1679)', *Oxford Dictionary of National Biography*, ed. H.C.G. Matthew and Brian Harrison, Oxford: Oxford University Press, 2004. http://www.oxforddnb.com.er.lib.ksu.edu/view/article/13400 (24 October 2005).

Martinich, A.P., *Hobbes: A Biography*, Cambridge: Cambridge University Press, 1999.

—— *The Two Gods of* Leviathan: *Thomas Hobbes on Religion and Politics*, New York: Cambridge University Press, 1992.

—— 'Thomas Hobbes', *Dictionary of Literary Biography, British Rhetoricians and Logicians, 1500–1660*, ed. Edward A. Malone., Vol. 281, Detroit: The Gale Group, 2003: 130–44. Literature Resource Center, Gale Group online database (subscription): http://galenet.galegroup.com.

Milner, Benjamin, 'Hobbes: On Religion', *Political Theory* 16.3 (August 1988): 400–25.

Mintz, Samuel, *The Hunting of* Leviathan: *Seventeenth Century Reactions to the Materialism and Moral Philosophy of Thomas Hobbes*, Cambridge: Cambridge University Press, 1962.

Mitchell, Joshua, 'Hobbes and the Equality of All under the One', *Political Theory* 21.3 (February 1993): 78–100.

—— 'Luther and Hobbes on the Question: Who Was Moses? Who Was Christ?', *The Journal of Politics* 53.3 (August 1991): 676–700.

Nagel, Thomas, 'Hobbes's Concept of Obligation', *The Philosophical Review* 61.1 (January 1959): 68–83.

Oakeshott, Michael, *Hobbes on Civil Association*, Berkeley: University of California Press, 1975.

Orwin, Clifford, 'On the Sovereign Authorization', *Political Theory* 3.1 (February 1975): 26–44.

Peters, Richard, *Hobbes*, Harmondsworth: Penguin Books, 1967.

Reilly, Susan P., 'Thomas Hobbes', *Dictionary of Literary Biography, British Philosophers, 1500–1799*, ed. Philip B. Dematteis and Peter S. Fosl, Vol. 252, Detroit: The Gale Group, 2001, pp. 182–94. Literature Resource Center, Gale Group online database (subscription): http://galenet.galegroup.com.

Schrock, Thomas S., 'The Rights to Punish and Resist Punishment in Hobbes' *Leviathan*', *The Western Political Quarterly* 44.4 (December 1991): 853–90.

Shulman, George, 'Hobbes, Puritans and Promethean Politics', *Political Theory* 16.3 (August 1988): 426–43.

Seaman, John W., 'Hobbes on Public Charity & the Prevention of Idleness: A Liberal Case for Welfare', *Polity* 23.1 (Autumn 1990): 105–26.

Shapiro, Barbara J., 'The Universities and Science in Seventeenth Century England', *The Journal of British Studies* 10.2 (May 1971): 47–82.

Simmons, John A., 'Locke's State of Nature', *Political Theory* 17.3 (August 1989): 449–70.

Skinner, Quentin, *Reason and Rhetoric in the Philosophy of* Leviathan, Cambridge: Cambridge University Press, 1996.

— 'The Ideological Context of Hobbes' Political Thought', *The Historical Journal* 9.3 (1966): 286–317.

Spragens, Thomas A. Jr., 'Hobbes on Civil Association', *The American Political Science Review* 72.2 (June 1978): 652–3.

Springborg, Patricia, 'Hobbes, Heresy and the Historia Ecclesiastica', *Journal of the History of Ideas* 55.4 (October 1994): 552–71.

— 'Hobbes's Biblical Beasts: Leviathan and Behemoth', *Political Theory* 23.2 (May 1995): 353–75.

State, Stephen, 'Hobbes and Hooker: Politics and Religion: A Note on the Structure of *Leviathan*', *Canadian Journal of Political Science* 20.1 (March 1987): 79–96.

Strauss, Leo, *The Political Philosophy of Hobbes: Its Basis and Its Genesis*, trans. Elsa M. Sinclair, Chicago: University of Chicago Press, 1984.

Strong, Tracy B., 'How to Write Scripture: Words, Authority, and Politics in Thomas Hobbes', *Critical Inquiry* 20.1 (Autumn 1993): 128–59.

Warrender, Howard, 'Political Theory and Historiography: A Reply to Professor Skinner of Hobbes', *The Historical Journal* 22.4 (December 1979): 931–40.

Watkins, J.W.N., 'The Posthumous Career of Thomas Hobbes', *The Review of Politics* 19.3 (July 1957): 351–60.

Wiener, Jonathan M., 'Quentin Skinner's Hobbes', *Political Theory* 2.3 (August 1974): 251–60.

# INDEX